Siroj Sorajjakool, Ph

Wu Wei, Negativity, and Depression
The Principle of Non-Trying in the Practice of Pastoral Care

Pre-publication
REVIEW

"**D**r. Sorajjakool has undertaken an ambitious task in his effort to join Western and Eastern thought in an understanding of depression. His bold attempt to examine the concept of *wu wei* in the context of Western philosophy is quite admirable. It is sometimes difficult for pastoral care professionals to move out of their usual theological thinking style as they try to help depressed individuals through 'doing.' The challenge of non-trying or *wu wei* not only allows pastoral care workers to indeed help the individual psychologically and existentially, but also allows them to get deeper, thus allowing the Spirit to work within and enriching the person spiritually. To be healed psychologically is also to deepen one's spiritual self."

C. Serena Gui, PhD
Psychologist;
Assistant Director,
Behavioral Medicine Faculty,
Florida Hospital Family Practice

Wu Wei, Negativity, and Depression

The Principle of Non-Trying in the Practice of Pastoral Care

THE HAWORTH PASTORAL PRESS
Rev. James W. Ellor, DMin, DCSW, CGP
Melvin A. Kimble, PhD
Co-Editors in Chief

Aging and Spirituality: Spiritual Dimensions of Aging Theory, Research, Practice, and Policy edited by David O. Moberg

Wu Wei, *Negativity, and Depression: The Principle of Non-Trying in the Practice of Pastoral Care* by Siroj Sorajjakool

Pastoral Care to Muslims: Building Bridges by Neville A. Kirkwood

Wu Wei, Negativity, and Depression

The Principle of Non-Trying in the Practice of Pastoral Care

Siroj Sorajjakool, PhD

The Haworth Pastoral Press®
An Imprint of The Haworth Press, Inc.
New York • London • Oxford

Published by

The Haworth Pastoral Press, an imprint of The Haworth Press, Inc., 10 Alice Street, Binghamton, NY 13904-1580

Cover design by Marylouise E. Doyle.

Library of Congress Cataloging-in-Publication Data

Sorajjakool, Siroj.
   Wu wei, negativity, and depression : the principle of non-trying in the practice of pastoral care / Siroj Sorajjakool.
      p. cm.
   Includes bibliographical references and index.
   ISBN 0-7890-1093-3 (alk. paper)—ISBN 0-7890-1094-1 (pbk. : alk. paper)
   1. Depressed persons—Pastoral counseling of. 2. Depression, Mental—Religious aspects—Christianity. 3 Depression, Mental —Religious aspects—Taoism. I. Title.

BV4461 .S67 2001
259'.425—dc21   00-050550

To my wife, Ling,
For believing
For everything

ABOUT THE AUTHOR

Siroj Sorajjakool, PhD, is Associate Professor of Religion (Pastoral Psychology) at Loma Linda University in California. He earned his PhD in Theology and Personality (Pastoral Care and Counseling) and his MA in Theological Studies at Claremont School of Theology. He also earned an MA in Religion from Andrews University. He was Associate Director of the Adventist Development and Relief Agency in Thailand and has served as a pastor in several churches.

CONTENTS

Foreword

Depression composes a world for those who suffer it. In that world, bleakness and blackness descend, as if forever. What could bring relief? The negativity of depression robs us of hope, zest, meaning, and a simple happiness in being. People dream of running and the ground under their feet heaves and falls away. An unarguable conviction presents itself, that sometime long ago, early in their lives, something went radically wrong and there is no fixing it. They are doomed to fail. They cannot live up to expectations or sustain simple happiness in being alive. Such suffering deepens into affliction of soul.

A fresh approach to remedy such distress is most welcome, especially one that recognizes a spiritual dimension of depression. Even in such distress a soul dwells. Depression itself may be another kind of door into reality that confers on us a sense that we belong, that we participate in a whole meaning that transcends our tiny perspective.

Here the author offers us the Eastern Taoist perception of *wu wei,* quite the opposite of our struggles in the West to achieve a sense of self that succeeds, strives, struggles, and aims to get more from life, however that element defines itself. We may seek money, power, justice, mental health, spiritual stature, fame, peace of mind and of world. Our values range from the most self-involved to the most exalted of human aspirations. Nonetheless, *wu wei* undermines them all. *Wu wei* climbs under the fence of Western divisions of better-worse, more-less good-evil.

Such dichotomies particularly torment those who suffer depression. They feel they fail—endlessly, constantly, hopelessly—to measure up to standards of what they should be and become. *Wu wei* states, in effect, that one should dig under these standards. Climb under the fence that imposes divisions on the self you are, compared to the self you should be. Empty yourself of all these criteria that we would impose on the flow of nature, trying to divide it up, colonize it, own it in self-designed plots. Making this mental and spiritual gesture of non-trying, this reduction to a level of self prior to all our constructions of yardsticks, the author brings clearly to the reader's attention that this does not mean opting out of life. It means simply disengaging from dichotomies, from preferring one opposite over another, which is doomed to failure because we thus split up life's flowing. Even our preference for being over nonbeing falls into this failure. Nonbeing is as much a part of living a lively life as is being. When we empty, open, "non-try," we enter a nondoing which leaves nothing undone, a doing that is effortless.

Readers can be grateful to the author for this fresh approach to the ancient affliction of depression. Dr. Sorajjakool gives us good understanding of what depression is, in all its aspects that oppress body, mind, and soul. The resources of the Way of *wu wei* introduce us to the subtlety and wisdom of Taoism and how it applies to the actual work with persons in the pain of depression. Finally, the author connects this spiritual tradition to the theology of Christianity. We are thus reminded that when we reach what I call the animal root-impulse of life and "the flow of nature," we see that what appear to be opposite traditions, in fact, belong to a whole reality that contains all our diversities.

Ann Belford Ulanov, PhD, LHD
Christiane Brooks Johnson Professor
of Psychiatry and Religion
Union Theological Seminary, NYC;
Psychoanalyst in private practice;
Faculty and Supervisor,
C.G. Jung Institute for Analytical Psychology, NYC

Preface

Depression is depressing. It discomforts. It invades. It sinks into the depth of one's soul. It devours one's spirit. When the spirit is empty, one becomes a "living dead." A living dead is a person who dies continually, still experiencing all the emotional pain. The "dead" person fights for life . . . fights for clarity in the midst of absurdity . . . fights for colors in the monochrome world and keeps fighting even as the shade of gray turns black. The monochrome world with faces in shades of black, white, and gray become one big dark cloud and the lines that distinguish faces blend into the dark horizon. I was there. I felt its monstrosity. I fought and felt its web tightening. And I asked myself, "Is there a way out of this downward spiral?" I begged for the promise "Take my yoke and follow me. For my yoke is easy and my burden is light." I prayed. In the distance I was drawn to the phrase "sitting down doing nothing." "Rest . . . Sabbath . . . " God's way is different from ours. If you want to go north, move south. If you want to go up, get down. If you want to move forward, step backward. I was fighting. God says, "Let go." In the distance I hear the phrase "sitting down doing nothing." What is written in this book is a journey toward that distant voice. It is a spiritual journey that I try to move toward within the scope of some technical language. To have substance, in this modern society, is to be able to substantiate through research and information. My deep wish is for readers to find—behind technicality—spirituality and the journey of the soul.

Depression may not be as pathological as we think. The voice in the distance that speaks through this melancholia may lead us to the soul. The journey is not toward the light at the end of the tunnel. It is light in the midst of the tunnel when we readjust the focus of our eyes. The path becomes clearer. The blind see what those with sight are unable to recognize. The monochrome world takes on a different type of color. Life emerges. In the midst of darkness God said, "Let there be light."

The journey into the discovery of the depth of spirituality through depression would have remained an impossibility without many individuals who assisted me in numerous ways from critiquing to cooking, from editing to paying bills, from discussing to nurturing. I wish to express my deep sense of gratitude to them for their help.

I wish to thank Dr. Kathleen Greider for her continued guidance in the understanding of the relationship between psychology and religion, and for thoughtful and constructive critiques and comments that have made this material coherent and organized. My interest in the area of social science that plays a major role in this book has been encouraged by Dr. Bill Clements. I have learned much about the importance of the biological aspects of psychology due to his continual encouragement. Dr. Stephen Kim played a significant role in clarifying concepts relating to Taoism and *wu wei*. Dr. Gerald Winslow spent a considerable amount of time discussing theological methods at length with me in the midst of his busy schedule. My interest in the concept of *wu wei* was deepened through philosophical discussion with Dr. Wesley Amundson.

There were also other friends who provided great encouragement in different ways. Some moaned with me. Some cooked for me. Some ate with me. Some talked to me. Thank you Dan Miller, Kwang Hee Park, Dagmar Grete, Janet Parachin, and Gabriel Mayer.

I owe much to two individuals for my firsthand clinical experience with depression. Wanda Lightfeldt, with whom I exchanged books, information, and experiences relating to clinical depression, gave me much insight into the cycle of depression. Catherine Allen offered me insights into her own experience with depression. I would like to thank both of them for their willingness to open themselves up as living human documents that reflect the journey with depression.

Elaine Walker and Kathleen Greider did a tremendous job in guiding me with form and style and in editing this manuscript. I am deeply appreciative. I also wish to thank Gayle Foster for her help in editing a part of this manuscript.

The last note of appreciation is reserved for the most important person in this whole process. I wish to express sincere gratitude to my wife, who knows that she truly deserves this. She has sacrificed much to make this a reality. She is the best!

Introduction

> Most people in the grip of depression at its ghastliest are, for whatever reason, in a state of unrealistic hopelessness, torn by exaggerated ills and fatal threats that bear no resemblance to actuality.
>
> William Styron

Depression is not only widespread but life threatening. It is estimated that in the course of a lifetime approximately 25 percent of the population will experience at least one major episode of depression and that, at any given moment, 9 to 20 percent of the population is experiencing symptoms of depression.[1] In reviewing epidemiological studies on depression, Martin E. P. Seligman concludes that the risk for people who were born in the last thirty years is ten times higher in comparison to those who were born seventy years ago.[2] He attributes this to the rise of individualism and the lack of commitment to something outside of oneself such as community or God.[3] Depression is not only prevalent but seems to be on the rise even in the face of a steep increase in research and therapeutic techniques for treating depression. Depression does not discriminate on the basis of faith. In a church of 100 adult members, at least 10 percent of the members are likely to be experiencing symptoms of depression.[4] What is worse, according to Gayle Belsher and Charles Costello, within two years of successful treatment, approximately 50 percent of this population will experience relapse.[5] Ian Gotlib and Constance Hammen comment, "Only recently have we come to understand that for many sufferers of major depression the disorder is recurrent, if not chronic."[6] David Karp, a sociologist, reflecting on his own experience of depression states, "For me, depression has a chronicity that makes it like a kind of mental arthritis; something that you just have to live with."[7]

The problems of chronicity and relapse have significant implications for pastoral caregivers. While there may be a general belief that appropriate treatment will cure depression, sufficient evidence does not substantiate this claim. A review of the research regarding psychotherapy for treatment of depression has shown that treated clients, even though they have improved, were still more depressed at the end of therapy than the nondepressed samples. The functioning level of depressed persons who received treatment is within one standard deviation lower than that of the general population, while those who did not receive treatment were functioning at two standard deviations below norm.[8] Further, even when they are treated, many will continue to experience symptoms of depression in a less intense form. Among these individuals, the struggle with negativity, one of the main symptoms of depression, will be central and continuous. In describing this struggle, Nina writes:

> When you are in it there is no more empathy, no intellect, no imagination, no compassion, no humanity, no hope. It isn't possible to roll over in bed because the capacity to plan and execute the required steps is too difficult to master, and the physical skills needed are too hard to complete . . .

> Depression steals away whoever you were, prevents you from seeing who you might someday be, and replaces your life with a black hole.[9]

In this experience of negativity that takes away hope, future, rationality, and the meaning of human existence, who will journey with those who suffer? Who will journey with them between their sessions with therapists or counselors, when the pain keeps recurring, when even successful treatments leave them with a residue of depressive symptoms, when medications run out, when, for economic reasons, they are no longer able to seek help from mental health professionals? In their continual struggle with negativity, who will journey with them?

Negativity takes away meaning and meaninglessness runs against the very core of our theology since meaning-making is the function of theology. As pastoral caregivers, we have the responsibility to help these people discover meaning or at least help them survive in the face of this dark abyss, this negativity. I believe this is where pastoral caregivers can play a significant role in the lives of depressed individuals, offering light in their existential darkness through sustaining ministry.

PROBLEM OF NEGATIVITY

Depression has the power to negate and to trap depressed individuals in a cycle of negativity. How can pastoral caregivers help depressed individuals cope with the negativity of depression so that they will be less trapped by its cycle?

Speaking of the self's ability to negate, sociologist Karp writes, "depression is a unique case since the most critical assaults on self come from within. . . . In the midst of an episode of depression individuals feel a self-hatred far greater than could possibly be expressed by others toward them." [10] These "critical assaults on self" are often accompanied by the desire to correct oneself through trying. To try is to set a goal toward which one strives. But this striving is always accompanied by the self's ability to negate itself.[11]

Striving and self-blame do not go hand in hand. Striving assumes that there is a self which one ought to be. Self-blame, on the other hand, is the autonomic script which keeps blaming the self for not having attained these goals. Hence, the more one strives, the further removed one is. This is how the negating power of negativity traps depressed individuals in its cycle. Through my counseling experience in a counseling center, an inpatient psychiatric facility, and with members of the church, I have observed that a vicious cycle is common among depressed individuals.

A close friend who is going through depression said to me, "I have been trying and trying and I get really tired of fighting. It is a cycle I don't seem to be able to get away from. I'm really sick of myself. I don't want to fight any more." I have heard similar phrases from others who have been through depression. Some fight the fear of rejection. Some fight the inordinate need for approval. Some fight a heightened level of self-consciousness. Some fight excessive amounts of unreasonable guilt. Some fight alienation. And many seem to realize that they are fighting something illogical where rationality has no control over emotion.

When the thought is triggered and the emotion stirred, the cycle spirals downward. People who are in this state often say, "I know it is illogical but I just can't stop it." They are caught in a cycle that does not seem to end. The trying keeps on even when the body experiences extreme fatigue. The deep wish is often expressed as "Please stop this spin and let me rest for a while." Yet one cannot help but keep on trying in an ocean of irrationality, wishing that perhaps just one more effort may lead to liberation from the vicious cycle. But the wish becomes a deeper pain. The yoke gets heavier. The downward spiral hits a new momentum.

How can depressed individuals remove themselves from this cycle of self-evaluation and self-criticism? Can pastoral caregivers help them cope with the negativity of depression so they will not be trapped in its cycle? Can we offer help to people who are tired of fighting, exhausted from trying, and get sick of themselves for not being able to attain their desired goals? I wonder if I can offer those in the midst of Hades the promise of Christ who said, "Take my yoke and follow me. For my yoke is easy and my burden is light." Is there a place where one who experiences this dark cycle of depression can rest awhile? Is there not a place where healing requires that one need not try a little harder? Is there a place of healing where the fight ceases and one just remains in exhaustion? Can there possibly be healing in just sitting in the face of negativity, fear, and despair? Can we just sit in Hades and let Heaven heal? I believe there is such a place. I would like to suggest that there is a tool Christians can add to the sustaining ministry of pastoral care that can help depressed individuals cope with the negativity of depression.

ARGUMENTS

The principle of *wu wei* (non-trying), as part of the sustaining function of pastoral care, can enhance depressed individuals' ability to cope with the negating power of the negativity of depression. This principle suggests that we need to align ourselves with the Way through emptying the self. Through this process, the principle of *wu wei,* helps reduce negativity's power to negate.

To argue this, I will first show that the experience of negativity leads one to try to affirm oneself through the process of self-evaluation. Second, the process of self-evaluation leads one to try to affirm oneself through self-regulation. In so doing, one gets caught in a cycle of self-regulatory perservation and self-criticism, because negativity negates every attempted self-regulation. Finally, the principle of *wu wei,* through emptying, stops this process of negation and allows a depressed person to exit the cycle of self-regulatory perseveration and self-criticism.

The first argument will point out how the experience of negativity leads one to seek self-affirmation. The path toward affirmation of the self is through self-worth, which is acquired through setting standards.[12] Standards lead to a gap between what this self is perceived to be and what it is thought the self ought to be. This discrepancy activates the process of self-regulation and leads to the effort of self-correction. "Only by engaging a self-regulatory cycle can one be certain that one is, indeed, valuable. Only by comparing oneself with standards can shortcomings in oneself be corrected."[13]

This argument will be supported by the self-regulatory perseveration theory of depression proposed by social psychologists Thomas Pyszczynski and Jeff Greenberg. In *Hanging On and Letting Go: Understanding the Onset, Progression, and Remission of Depression* (1992), Pyszczynski and Greenberg state that this theory differs from other theories of depression in that, instead of "viewing depression as the result of the individual generally giving up on goals, we view it as the result of the individual failing to give up on an unobtainable goal when it would be adaptive to do so."[14]

My second argument will deal with the relationship between trying and the inability to exit the cycle of depression. To try is to suggest that what is, is not good enough. To try to move from the feeling that I am not good enough to the place where I ought to be is to pursue the illusion of a self, of the ghost, because it is not possible to affirm through negation. According to self-regulatory perseveration theory, depression is the condition whereby one is unable to close the gap between the "is" and the "ought" and at the same time, experiences the inability to exit this self-regulatory process. One keeps trying to obtain the standards by which one judges one's value and worth. This attempt only increases the focus on oneself. This increased focus and the inability to close the gap intensifies the negative affect. "The intensified negative affect, self-blame, self-evaluation, and disruption of successful, competent behavior in other domains pushes the recently destabilized self-concept toward negativity."[15] The recovery process, according to Pyszczynski and Greenberg, is in giving up the definition one assigns to meaning and worth since this definition is unattainable by the self.[16]

Third, I will argue that the principle of *wu wei,* through emptying, stops the process of negation and thus allows a depressed person to exit the cycle of self-perseveration and self-criticism. According to Pyszczynsnki and Greenberg, depressed individuals need to be brought to the realization that the goal which they strive to attain is unattainable. At the same time they need to acquire an alternative source of self-worth. Only when they are able to redefine their goals can they achieve their self-worth and deactivate self-focused attention. When the attention is not focused on the self, the gap is closed and one is able to exit the cycle. This similar process is taught by Chuang Tzu and Lao Tzu.

Chuang Tzu and Lao Tzu teach that the more one tries the more one becomes alienated from oneself. Every "try" reduces the self. The path toward authentic selfhood is reduction of effort. It is to try by not trying. *Wu wei* invites us to return to the authentic self through the method of reduction. It invites us to life through the process of emptying because life is a paradox. Movement forward may be achieved by stepping backward. Lao Tzu writes, "The path into the light seems dark, the path forward seems to go back."[17] Pastoral caregivers can help depressed people by offering them this principle of *wu wei* because in emptying, there are no constructed standards. When there is no standard there is nothing to negate. The process of negation ceases. This is the way of non-doing; the way of *wu wei.*

LIMITATIONS

Because of the extensive amount of literature on depression in various disciplines, it is essential to state clearly the scope and limitations of this study. Parts of this book will include discussions of etiology, biological theories, psychosocial theories, and treatment of depression, but these are not the main focus of this study. The main focus is the problem of the negativity of depression and its destructive power to negate. While a depressed individual struggles with the negativity of depression and undergoes other forms of treatment, how can pastoral caregivers enhance his or her ability to cope? This book sees *wu wei* as a principle that can be used concurrently with other counseling techniques, psychotherapies, and/or psychotropic medications.

As a book on pastoral care, the population it addresses consists of pastoral caregivers in parishes and chaplaincy. It assumes some basic understanding of pastoral care, pastoral counseling, and pastoral theology.

It is also important to acknowledge the complexity of the concepts of Tao and *wu wei*. These are deep philosophical concepts to grasp, and I do not claim to have an in-depth understanding. What I try to describe in this book are aspects of these concepts that I find helpful and applicable to the practice of pastoral care for depressed individuals. Explanation of the concepts of *wu wei* and *Tao* will be limited primarily to available English translations and commentaries.

CONTRIBUTION TO PASTORAL CARE

This study will help to expand the understanding of the mechanism that traps depressed individuals in its cycle, by using the principle of *wu wei* and the theory of self-regulatory perseveration. It will also show how, by applying this religious principle, depressed individuals can slowly reduce the negating power of negativity and step out of this debilitating cycle of depression. It is also my hope that by introducing another coping skill, the work of pastoral caregivers among depressed individuals may be enhanced. Finally, this study sees depression as an attempt of the psyche to direct the self toward wholeness and spirituality. *Wu wei* is not just a method, but implies a redefinition of the self rooted in spirituality.

ORGANIZATION OF THE BOOK

This book begins with the problem of depression, moves through the mechanics of the negativity of depression, explains the place of *wu wei* as a way out, and concludes with a theological statement in an attempt to show that this principle does not contradict the theological basis of pastoral care. The rationale for placing the theological basis of pastoral care at the end is so readers will have an understanding of the concept of nonbeing in *wu wei* before touching on the significance of this concept in theology.

Chapter 1 offers a criteria and existential descriptions of depression, followed by a discussion on epidemiology that covers lifetime prevalence, gender differences, age of onset, recurrence, and ends with a brief history of the understanding of depression.

Causes of depression are discussed in Chapter 2. Here I look at psychosocial theories of depression such as the role of stressors and the place of interpretation. The second part of the chapter deals with the biological basis of depression. What is said in this section only reflects an attempt at understanding the biological basis of depression.

Chapter 3 aims at providing readers with an overview of the approaches to the problem of melancholy and depression in the practice of pastoral care. It looks at different types of interventions in the past and in contemporary practice of pastoral care and counseling. The chapter ends with my reflection on the relationship of these various interventions and the principle of *wu wei* (the similarities and differences). The intention of this chapter is to provide a context for the discussion of the principle of *wu wei* in the practice of pastoral care.

The relationship between negativity and trying is discussed in Chapter 4. This chapter starts with the place of negativity among depressed individuals and the impact this negativity has on different aspects of life. The second part shows how the experience of negativity becomes the driving force that pushes depressed individuals to try to overcome negativity.

Chapter 5 shows how this "trying," or self-regulatory perseveration, leads to the downward spiral whereby one is caught in a cycle of trying to overcome negativity and yet being trapped by its power to negate. The solution I wish to offer for people who are caught within this web is contained in the principle of *wu wei,* which is discussed in Chapter 6.

In Chapter 7, the connection between trying and *wu wei* is explained. It contains a deeper analysis of the concept of *wu wei* in relation to "trying," through the terms prereductive, reductive, and postreductive self according to Kuang-ming Wu.

Chapter 8 provides a closer analysis of the principle of *wu wei* in the context of depression, which shows how the application of this principle can help one exit the cycle of negativity. It also aims at showing the place of *wu wei* in the sustaining ministry of pastoral care. The practical applications of these principles are explained in Chapter 9. Chapter 10 is an attempt at answering the questions "Can this principle, which is based on Taoist philosophy, be utilized by pastoral caregivers? Can pastoral theology accommodate this principle of *wu wei* and remain faithful to its calling?"

Chapter 1

Overview of the Problem
of Depression

Depression is an insidious vacuum that crawls into your brain and pushes your mind out of the way. It is the complete absence of rational thought. It is freezing cold, with a dangerous, horrifying, terrifying fog wafting throughout whatever is left of your mind.

Unemployed female, age 27

My God, my God, why have you forsaken me? Why are you so far from saving me, so far from the words of my groaning? O my God, I cry out by day, but you do not answer, by night, and am not silent.

King David, Psalms 22:1, 2 (NIV)

NARRATIVES

Siroj

My encounter with depression started with a series of stressful events around mid-1993. I had been under stress for three months due to a work situation that created conflicted feelings within me. The event that initiated me fully into clinical depression, however, took place in September. I received a phone call from a friend around 6:30 a.m. and was informed that, according to the 5:00 morning news, my Aunt Sansiri's house had caught fire earlier that morning. I grew up spending lots of time with her and her family. I was shocked by the news and immediately rushed to pick up this friend before heading toward my aunt's home. On the way I kept thinking about what I could do to help relocate my Aunt Sansiri, my cousin, my cousin's husband, and their two daughters (a three-year-old and an eight-month-old). In my mind I pictured many other houses in the vicinity being burnt as well, and the occupants standing in front of them with luggage and whatever other belongings they could save from the fire. Before we arrived, my friend, with some hesitation in her voice, told me very quietly that, according to the news, a few deaths had resulted from this fire. I did not pay much attention. When I pulled my car in front of Aunt Sansiri's house I saw sixty to seventy people gathered around her house—the only house that was consumed by fire. I heard neighbors say, "We heard women screaming for help but there was nothing we could do." This tragic accident took the lives of Aunt Sansiri, my cousin, her husband, and my nieces. I sat in front of the house with tears swelling in my eyes but fought to keep control. I did not want to cry in front of my friend. I wanted to look strong, but I was all broken up inside.

The following week, I spent a major portion of my time at the hospital identifying the charred bodies and completing the necessary paperwork, arranging the funeral service, meeting relatives, arranging for compensation for the two domestic helpers that died in the fire, etc. I did not have time to process my own feelings.

Exactly one month later I started developing strange feelings. I could not understand what was going on with me. My energy level dropped drastically, and I had a very difficult time getting up in the morning. I was unable to sleep and I found myself staying awake until three or four in the morning. I would watch two or three movies in the night just to pass the time. One night while lying in bed I felt a deep sense of sadness and asked my wife to please hold me. With her arms around me, I sobbed and sobbed. She asked me what was happening, but I could not tell her. A few words that came to my mind were despair, doom, and hopelessness.

An incredible darkness invaded my life. I could not concentrate. Every recollection of the past was dreadful. My thoughts were racing and I could not stop them. I kept asking myself why I could not snap out of it, but that was not an option. I wondered what had happened to my faith. Many nights I found myself praying for God to please take this away from me but to no avail. The feeling of guilt was overwhelming. Every little misdeed could trigger an inordinate amount of guilt. I went to see three physicians and told them my extreme fatigue and these strange sensations. None could tell me what was wrong, and this further complicated my problem. It was not until I came to the Claremont School of Theology and registered for the course, "Diagnostic Studies in Psychiatry and Religion," that I finally understood my problem.

Sandra

Sandra came to Loma Linda Behavioral Medicine Center one day without an appointment. Her close friend had just died. Sandra was suicidal. She was hoping to see someone, but after a long wait, Sandra walked out. At the door she met a counselor who noticed that Sandra was in deep emotional pain. "Don't go now," said the counselor. "You need to talk to someone. I will get you in to talk to the chaplain." That was the first of many meetings with Sandra, during which she revealed her life story.

When Sandra was seven years old her mother often left her with her grandfather, who was a convicted pedophile and had been incarcerated. Although her mother was well aware of this situation, she continued to leave Sandra with him. For the next two years Sandra suffered sexual molestation by her grandfather.

When she was ten her father molested her. Sandra recalled the many nights she stared out the window looking at the stars. "I learned to dissociate myself while he was doing it," said Sandra. "I wasn't there." She also remembered the extreme rage of her father and the script that is still operant in her subconscious mind, "You are bad. You are worth nothing. You are a piece of shit!" Many nights when her father came home she would hear him say, "Wipe that look off your face!" She did not know what that look was and did not know how to change her expression. Getting beaten for it was a common experience for her. She could do no right. "There was one thing I did well," said Sandra. "I was a very good student. My parents never saw my report cards nor cared to see them. In fact they were upset that I received awards from school." She was told when she came home with good grades that she was arrogant and that she brought shame to the family.

One day, as an adolescent, when she arrived home from school she saw a yellow cordon around the house, with an ambulance, police cars, and many people gathered around. She was told as she walked toward the house that her dad had shot himself in the heart. "There was blood all over the kitchen area and I was very scared," recalled Sandra.

At the age of nineteen she got married and quickly became pregnant. Less than a year after her marriage, someone cut in front of her car on the freeway. The accident left her in a coma for three days. The impact of the accident caused the baby to be aborted. After coming out of the coma, she went through many operations for the reconstruction of her cheekbones. A brain scan showed a very low level of neurotransmitters, which made her more vulnerable to depression. Since the accident, Sandra had been in therapy for over twenty years trying to deal with her grief and depression. During the course of treatment she was sexually molested by one of her psychotherapists.

Sandra's family had a history of psychiatric symptoms. Her maternal grandfather suffered from depression and was hospitalized for a long time. Her mother was diagnosed with anxiety disorder and Sandra's eldest daughter is presently experiencing depression. Sandra's father had a history of depression as well as a heart condition, and ultimately committed suicide.

Besides her family history and her traumatic childhood experience, she had gone through two divorces (her first husband was very controlling and abusive). Sandra complains of "blue days" without any trigger. Every ordinary daily task becomes a huge performance that takes extraordinary effort. "I hate it when people tell me 'Why can't you just snap out of it?' You can't snap out of depression. You just can't!" mourned Sandra.

THE MEANING OF DEPRESSION

We all encounter depression at some point in our lives. We use the term depression to describe instances when we do not perform well on our examinations, when we get into an argument with our spouse, or when conflict occurs at our workplace. This type of depression is very different from clinical depression. The clinically depressed person, according to Dayringer, is the person who is "so depressed as to have physiological symptoms."

The benchmark for clinical depression, compared to normal sadness, depends on the intensity, severity, and duration of symptoms. Generally, if the depressed mood and associated symptoms last for more than two weeks, and if they are of sufficient intensity to interfere with ordinary daily activities, this is considered a clinical depressive syndrome.[2]

Gotlib and Hammen define clinical depression as "depressed mood along with a set of additional symptoms persisting over time, and causing disruption and impairment of functioning."[3]

David Karp, after interviewing fifty persons in treatment for depression, identified four stages that most people experience: (1) a period where they do not have the vocabulary to describe their experience of depression; (2) a phase where they realize that something is really wrong with them; (3) a crisis stage that thrusts them into the hands of therapists; and (4) a phase where they come to accept their illness identity.[4]

In the *Diagnostic and Statistical Manual of Mental Disorders* (DSM-IV), depression is an Axis I diagnosis, which is categorized as a mood disorder. Although mood disorders include depressive disorders, bipolar disorders, mood disorder due to a general medical condition, and substance-induced mood disorder, this book is limited to only the understanding of depressive disorders (major depressive disorder, dysthymic disorder and depressive disorder not otherwise specified). The diagnosis criteria for major depressive episode are:

A. Five (or more) of the following symptoms have been present during the same 2-week period and represent a change from previous functioning; at least one of the symptoms is either (1) depressed mood or (2) loss of interest or pleasure.

1. depressed mood most of the day, nearly every day, as indicated by either subjective report (e.g., feels sad or empty) or observation made by others (e.g., appears tearful). Note: In children and adolescents, can be irritable mood.
2. markedly diminished interest or pleasure in all, or almost all, activities most of the day, nearly every day (as indicated by either subjective account or observation made by others).
3. significant weight loss when not dieting or weight gain (e.g., a change of more than 5 percent of body weight in a

month), or decrease or increase in appetite nearly every day. Note: In children, consider failure to make expected weight gains.

4. insomnia or hypersomnia nearly every day.

5. psychomotor agitation or retardation nearly every day (observable by others, not merely subjective feelings of restlessness or being slowed down).

6. fatigue or loss of energy nearly every day.

7. feelings of worthlessness or excessive or inappropriate guilt (which may be delusional) nearly every day (not merely self-reproach or guilt about being sick).

8. diminished ability to think or concentrate, or indecisiveness, nearly every day (either by subjective account or as observed by others).

9. recurrent thoughts of death (not just fear of dying), recurrent suicidal ideation without a specific plan, or a suicide attempt or a specific plan for committing suicide.

B. The symptoms do not meet criteria for a Mixed Episode.

C. The symptoms cause clinically significant distress or impairment in social, occupational, or other important areas of functioning.

D. The symptoms are not due to the direct physiological effects of a substance (e.g., a drug of abuse, a medication) or a general medical condition (e.g., hypothyroidism).

E. The symptoms are not better accounted for by Bereavement, i.e., after the loss of a loved one, the symptoms persist for longer than two months or are characterized by marked functional impairment, morbid preoccupation with worthlessness, suicidal ideation, psychotic symptoms, or psychomotor retardation.[5]

Kaplan and Sadock provide a useful narrative description of depression:

A depressed mood and a loss of interest or pleasure are the key symptoms of depression. Patients may say that they feel blue, hopeless, in the dumps, or worthless. For the patient the depressed mood often has a distinct quality that differentiates it from the normal emotion of sadness or grief. Patients often describe the symptom of depression as one of agonizing emotional pain.[6]

With all the diagnostic and assessment tools that have been accumulated through studies and research, one of the most striking observations I have made among patients who suffer from depression is their inability to articulate and describe the experience of depression that has been exacerbated by the lack of existential understanding of the meaning of depression within the society. A female graduate student once described this inexpressible darkness of depression: "It's the worst feeling in the world. It's right where my heart is. I don't know if you can feel . . . yah, you can feel emptiness. Like there's a black hole there. I'll tell you, it's the scariest thing. . . . You can't talk about your depression with people who don't experience it. They don't understand."[7] To try to understand depression without experiencing it is just like trying to understand hunger analytically while sitting in a nice restaurant. People just "don't get it!" For pastoral caregivers trying to help depressed patients/clients, one of the most important gifts we can offer is to invite them to describe their feelings and assist them in their articulation.

EPIDEMIOLOGY

The following sections will address the issues of who is being affected, gender differences, the age of onset, the possibility for recurrence or relapse, and the duration of depression.

Lifetime Prevalence

The wide prevalence of depression in modern society has given rise to what Gerald Klerman calls "the age of melancholy." The Epidemiological Catchment Area (ECA) study sponsored by the National Institute of Mental Health between 1980-1982, after interviewing over 9,500 people in three sites (New Haven, Baltimore, and St. Louis), showed a significant increase in the rate of depression between people who were born around 1960 and those born during World War I. Those born in 1960 have a 5 to 6 percent probability rate of experiencing an episode of depression while those born during World War I have a rate of only 1 percent.[8]

A study by Klerman showed an even higher increase in the rate of depression. According to the epidemiological study[9] based on the same design as the ECA[10] study but with a different sample (2,289 first-degree relatives of 523 people who were diagnosed with major affective disorder), "if you are thirty years old and you were born around 1950 your risk is about 60 percent, whereas your great-grandmother's risk for depression was about 3 percent by the time she reached thirty."[11]

According to Myrna Weissman and J. Myers' survey in 1978, the lifetime prevalence in the United States population for a major depressive disorder was 18 percent. This figure implies that over a lifetime, 12 percent of men and 26 percent of women can be expected to develop major depressive disorder.[12]

In 1981, Weissman and Jeffrey Boyd's research showed the lifetime prevalence between 8 and 12 percent for men and 20 to 26 percent for women in the United States.[13]

Gotlib and Hammen believe that the lifetime prevalence is approximately 25 percent for the general population and 75 percent for all psychiatric hospitalizations and that each year more than 100 million people worldwide experience the symptoms of clinical depression.[14]

It is estimated that approximately 20 million people may suffer serious depression from time to time and only a few of them receive help. This implies that "during any six-month period, as many as 10 million Americans find themselves sliding into the black hole of depression."[15] Of those who suffer depression, only one in five receives treatment and one in fifty is hospitalized. It is estimated that one in 100 commits suicide.[16] An average physician, during the lifetime of his or her practice, will have fourteen patients who commit suicide and as many as 10 percent will see their physicians on the day or just prior to the day of their suicide.[17] Because of the widespread effects of this illness on individuals, Gotlib and Catherine Colby say depression is "the single most common psychiatric disorder seen by mental health professionals and is perhaps the most lethal."[18]

Gender

The global study on lifetime range of prevalence showed a 2 to 12 percent possibility for men and a 5 to 26 percent for women. All the studies seem to suggest that women's risk for unipolar depression is twice as high than for men.[19] According to John Wing and Paul Bebbington the "rates for women are higher than those for men at virtually all ages," while the pattern of distribution by age is quite different.[20] Many researchers believe that the reason unipolar depression is twice as high among women than men is because of the construction of patriarchy and sexism in society. [21] Women have been taught that to be good is to be passive, dependent, and helpless. When they are strong and independent, they are bad. The internalization of these messages leads to the depletion of the self, which ultimately results in clinical depression. Perhaps it is for this reason that Christie Neuger writes: "Women and men live in a culture that is powerfully depressogenic for women."[22]

Another theory sees gender differences as a result of coping styles. Nolen-Hoeksema believes that the high ratio of depression among women is because of their tendency to ruminate.[23] Rumination refers to the tendency to ponder over issues and problems by analyzing and trying to fix them. This tendency to ruminate is based on the theory of learned helplessness, whereby one's explanatory style, which correlates negatives with internal causes, results in a sense of helplessness.[24]

Age of Onset

There are various opinions on the age of onset for depression. A number of studies seem to recognize that early age of onset for depression is on the rise. Peter Lewinsohn, Edward Duncan, Alyn Stanton, and Martin Hautzinger's study based on 2,046 subjects who met the criteria for depression according to the Center for Epidemiological Studies Depressive Scale (CES-D) found that onsets were low in childhood, increased drastically in adolescence, peaked during middle age, and decreased sharply among the elderly population. In relation to gender, there is no difference before the age of nine and after sixty-nine. For males, the rate increases at twenty and stabilizes throughout adulthood, but may peak at forty-five to forty-nine. For females, the risk increases during adolescence and continues during adulthood until the rate peaks at approximately fifty years of age. The risk decreases after fifty for both males and females.[25]

According to the Los Angeles Epidemiological Catchment Area study (1991), 25 percent reported that they experienced major depression during childhood or adolescence while 50 percent reported onset by the age of twenty-five.

Reflecting on these studies, Gotlib and Hammen write, "depression appears to be a disorder of relatively younger onset than in the past, with particular risk in late adolescence and early adulthood."[26]

It is not uncommon for children or the elderly to be diagnosed with major depression. Some recent data show an increasing rate of depression among persons under twenty.[27] According to Weissman, an international study of depression showed that in each successive generation, major depression began at an earlier stage. The rationales cited to explain this phenomena are: (a) marked increase in divorce rate; (b) a decrease in the time available for children in the family; (c) industrial substances released into the air; and (d) decline in religious belief.[28] The increase in the rate of depression also affects the geriatric population. Studies on geriatric depression found that this illness affects 25 percent of the population.[29]

The early age of onset of depression, in comparison to what was once known as the disorder of middle age, and the widespread extent of this illness seem to correspond with Seligman's argument that the increased risk for depression for this generation is connected to the doctrine of individualism and the loss of religious values in our present society. The loss of religious values here refers to increased dependency on self and the lack of a sustaining belief system.[30]

Recurrence and Relapse

Studies of patients admitted for the treatment of depression show that only 5 to 15 percent have a single episode and a study of outpatients on maintenance therapy indicated that only 20 percent had a single episode. Recurrence is thus an important issue in the treatment of unipolar affective disorder.[31]

A number of studies on relapse provide interesting clues that help us understand factors contributing to relapse among depressed individuals. Based on a study of seventy-five patients who recovered from depression during an eight-week treatment program, Martin Keller, Robert Shapiro, Philip Lavori, and Nicola Wolfe reported a 24 percent rate of relapse within twelve weeks and 12 percent within the first four weeks.[32] A study carried out a year after treatment on sixty-six patients who recovered from chronic minor depression showed that 36 percent of these patients relapsed into major affective disorder.[33] According to "The Consensus Development Conferences Statement," as many as 50 percent of recovered patients experience relapse within the first two years and the likelihood of recurrence is greatest during the first four to six months after recovery.[34]

After reviewing a number of studies on relapse, Belsher and Costello conclude by pointing to factors that may contribute to relapse. These are (a) recent environmental stress; (b) absence of social support; (c) a history of depressive episodes; (d) persistent neuroendocrine dysregulation after recovery; and (e) withdrawal of medication.[35]

Duration and Frequency of Illness

It is believed that, in general, the duration of depression is between four to eight months.[36] The usual course of depression is often the recurrence of depression separated by intervals of several symptom-free years. Some patients have annual depressions during a specific season, while others suffer intermittently. The mean number of episodes in depression is five to six, but the best predictor of recurrence is the previous course. If the patient has three episodes in two years, chances are that patient will repeat the same pattern. It is believed that between 10 to 20 percent of depressed patients will have a chronic course.[37] Factors contributing to the chronic course of depression include a history of affective disorder, early-onset of dysthymia, environmental stress, and inadequate treatment.[38]

HISTORY OF THE STUDIES OF DEPRESSION

The following short review of the historical development of the understanding of depression reflects the tension between biological and psychological explanations of the cause of depression. Ancient history viewed depression as a curse from the gods and a sign of weakness, while the first clinician, Hippocrates (400 B.C.), believed psychiatric problems originated in the brain. Hence the terms "mania" and "melancholia" were associated with mental disturbances. Aulus Cornelius Celsus (30 A.D.) believed that depression was caused by black bile.[39] As early as the second century, Aretaeus of Cappadocia recognized organic (endogenous) and external (situational) depressions as two types of illnesses. He also recognized the difference between unipolar depression and episodes of both depression and mania.

The Dark Ages (476-1000 A.D.) witnessed the return of Western civilization to the belief in the supernatural as the etiology of psychiatric disorders. The move from supernatural to natural explanation was initiated by the Renaissance. Johann Weyer (1515-1588), a sixteenth century physician, linked depression with bodily symptoms. The concept of suicide as a manifestation of despair was first recognized by Timothy Bright, a British physician, around the same period. In *Anatomy of Melancholy* (1630), Robert Burton showed how the progression from natural grief at death or separation leads to depression.[40] In 1882, the term "cyclothymia" was used by German psychiatrist Karl Kahlbaum to describe mania and depression as stages of the same illness.[41]

The late nineteenth and twentieth centuries witnessed a movement toward descriptive diagnosis (based on specific signs and symptoms) and unconscious factors. Sigmund Freud (1856-1939) based his understanding of depression on the development of personality. Depression is an attempt at intrapsychic repair in which a person punishes himself or herself for the loss of a loved one. It is a "form of self-reproaches to the effect that the mourner himself is to blame for the loss of the loved object."[42] It is anger turned on the self. Birbring, a twentieth-century psychoanalyst, saw the loss of self-esteem as a common denominator among depressed individuals. Early psychoanalytic thinkers came to realize that perhaps depression could be accounted for not only by anger turning toward self or the loss of self-esteem, but by many other factors as well. In the 1950s, antidepressant medications such as monoamine oxidase inhibitors and tricyclic antidepressants were first introduced. Greater emphasis was placed on the biological aspect of depression. The 1970s witnessed a new class of antidepressants such as selective serotonin reuptake inhibitors (SSRIs).[43]

Chapter 2

Psychosocial and Biological
Theories of Depression

Depression, then, is a result of the dysregulated interaction of feedback mechanisms at the experiential, neurochemical, and behavioral levels.

Robert Hedaya

Although conflicting opinions exist about the role of external stressful events on depression, most clinicians agree that a correlation occurs between stressful life events and depression. Describing his interviews with fifty patients who had experienced major depressive episodes, Karp states that "nearly everyone could pinpoint the precise time, situation, or set of events that moved them from the recognition that something was wrong to the realization that they were desperately sick."[1] Most of these patients could recall with vivid detail when things got out of hand.

Clinical observation indicates that "stressful life events more often precede the first episodes of mood disorders than subsequent episodes."[2] This is true for both major depressive episode and bipolar I disorder. It is proposed that the stressful events a person experiences cause long-lasting changes in the functioning of neurotransmitter and intraneuronal signaling systems. The changes may even include loss of neurons and an excessive reduction in synaptic contacts. For this reason, the revisiting of the following depressive episodes may take place without an external stressor.[3]

LIFE EVENTS AND STRESSORS

In her article "Prevalence and Course of Affective Disorders," Clayton identifies factors affecting the accuracy of the study of the relationship between depression and life events. Depressed patients, suggests Clayton, are prone toward inaccuracies of recall. Further, life events that cause stress can be the result of depressive symptoms in patients. For example, poor job performance may be the result of depression and vice versa. The symptoms that meet the criteria for major depressive episodes may be regarded as normal response to loss.[4]

Different types of events may lead to the experience of depression. These are bereavement, economic difficulties, lack of social support, marital distress, and gender roles. Andrew Billings and Rudolf Moos point out that negative life events in the areas of health, finances, interpersonal relationships and losses "are three to six times more common among depressed individuals as compared to demographically matched general population controls."[5] Speaking of lack of family support as a psychosocial factor, Billings and Moos identify three characteristics found among the families of depressed patients: (1) less cohesion; (2) less interpersonal expressiveness; and (3) more conflict. Patients who lack family cohesion with less interpersonal expression tend to get into more conflicts that create stress and tension.[6]

Loss

Interest in psychosocial factors and depression has directed the attention of researchers to the area of early losses through death or separation.[7] The life events that are most associated with a later development of depression are the loss of a parent before the age of eleven and the loss of a spouse.[8] However, other investigators did not find correlation between early loss and depression. Although it may not be possible to draw firm conclusions regarding this matter, clinicians need to be sensitive to the issue of early loss and its possible relation to depression.[9] The conflicting results in the study of early loss also led researchers to explore the relationship between the role of parental care and depression. Tirril Harris, George W. Brown, and A. Bifulco found that early maternal loss does not predict onset of depression in adulthood when adequate parental care is evident.[10] A study on early parental behavior by Thomas Crook, Allen Raskin, and John Eliot found that depressed individuals often described their parents as rejecting, controlling, hostile, detached, and instilling persistent anxiety.[11]

Economic Difficulties

Researchers have found consistent reports that show correlation between people in the low socioeconomic classes and depressive disorders with the exception of people with bipolar disorder (which is a disorder of stronger correlation with higher economic status). Women with children who have low-income and low-status jobs have a higher risk of developing clinical depression.[12]

Social Support

A major epidemiological study of depressive symptomatology by Brown and Harris found that people who experience close, confiding relationships are less likely to experience clinical depression when faced with stressful life events, in comparison to those who lack such social support. Brown and Harris also identified three common stressful factors that increase the risk for depression among women: (1) unemployment; (2) having three or more children at home; and (3) the loss of the mother before the age of eleven.[13]

Another study that focuses on the quality and quantity of relationships in predicting depression was done by S. Henderson, D. G. Byrne, and P. Duncan-Jones in Australia. This study shows that depressed individuals have as much contact with family members as nondepressed individuals. The difference is in the quality of the relationships. Depressed individuals' interpersonal relations were experienced as affectively unpleasant.[14]

Marital Distress

The relationship between marital distress and depression has been well documented. Weissman's study reported that 45.5 percent of depressed women experienced marital distress.[15] Frederic W. Ilfeld found that 25 percent of depression scores in a community survey were related to stresses of marriage and parenting.[16] Lars Freden's study based on 91 depressed men and women and 109 nondepressed individuals in Sweden found that 40 percent of depressed individuals reported the lack of communication while only 7 percent of nondepressed individuals reported similar communication problems.[17]

Gender Roles

Many attempts have been made to understand the high rate of depression among women. Feminist pastoral theologians such as Dunlap and Neuger recognize the importance of social environment and its effect on the experience of depression among women. It is believed that one-third of women have been abused sexually during childhood, one-fourth to one-half have been battered, while three-fourths have been sexually harassed at work. Besides the abuse that they experience, women are ascribed social roles that can serve to foster depressive tendencies. In addressing this issue Dunlap writes:

> Dependence, helplessness, passivity, accommodation, self-sacrifice — all of these qualities are considered feminine in our culture and all of them have been identified as conducive to depression. To relinquish a sense of agency and control, to mold one's feelings and opinions to those around you, to see one's worth as derivative of those you serve, all of these are part of this culture's definition of the feminine and all of them are clinically depressogenic.[18]

STRESSORS AND INTERPRETATION

Although there seems to be a correlation between stressful life events and depression, it is not clear how stressful life events affect the development of depression in individuals. Gotlib and Hammen suggest five models for the understanding of the psychosocial factors affecting depression.

1. Barbara Dohrenwend's model establishes the connection between negative life events and depression. Her research shows that depressed patients experienced a greater number of stressors in a year prior to the episode. The categories of stressors are loss, illness or injury, and events that disrupt social support.[19]
2. Richard Lazarus and Susan Folkman place emphasis on the appraisal of events as a determinant of the impact of stressors.

Stressors, therefore, cannot be measured using objective check-lists but through subjective appraisal of events.[20]

3. Brown and Harris's studies point to the importance of contexts in the understanding of depression (the relationship between events and difficulties, the level of commitment to the role, and role conflict).[21]

4. Lewinsohn and Moos view stressors as one of the ingredients among many others that include family support and cognitive and coping styles.[22]

5. Cognitive theory suggests a cognitive vulnerability that is activated by stressful events.[23]

While debate continues in the discussion of the relationship between life events and depression, it is adequate to state that among these theories one finds common factors such as the existence of stressors and the role of cognition or interpretation. In discussing her biopsychosocial model of depression, Dunlap believes that humans are constantly trying to make meaning of their existence. In their encounter with stressful events, stress is mediated through their interpretive lens. Hence, whether or not an event is a stressor depends on the meaning given to that particular event.[24]

For Dunlap, events in themselves do not have the power to cause depression. It is the interpretation of these events both at conscious and unconscious levels that plays an important role in developing the symptoms of depression. What do people see through the lens that can be depressive? A number of studies seem to suggest that depression sets in when the events (both internal and external) are interpreted as loss for the self. This loss includes the loss of meaning, purpose, hope, and self-esteem.

After reviewing studies on the relationship between environmental factors and depression, Gotlib and Hammen point to loss as a common factor. Speaking of the need to expand the definition of loss, they write:

> It is argued that the key psychological ingredient determining whether someone will experience depression following a negative event is the appraisal of the meaning of the event as signaling loss of self-worth, a belief that something essential for one's

experience of being valued has been lost with no means of re-placing it.[25]

SYNAPSES AND CNS NEUROTRANSMITTERS

Human beings are physically composed, yet we transcend all physical objects. We possess life, vitality, emotion, and the ability to think. What initiates this physics into a thinking and feeling human being remains a mystery. We have come to call this physics and its physiological functioning "me" or "myself." This implies that thinking and feelings are chemical. As such, the experience of depression, too, has its chemical components. What is the mechanism of depression that results in the feeling of emptiness and negativity? Central to the biological theory of depression is the interrelationship between synapses, neurotransmitters, and the CNS (central nervous system).

Synapses and CNS

Impulses are transmitted from one neuron to another across a synapse (a junction between the cells). Disruption of the synaptic communication is one of the main causes of most diseases of the brain. Synapses are also the site of action for most drugs that affect the brain. There are two types of synapses: electrical and chemical. Electrical synapses pass nerve impulses from one neuron to another through small, tubular, protein structures called gap junctions. Chemical synapses secrete chemical substances called neurotransmitters that act on receptors of the next neuron.[26] The synapses in the CNS are strictly chemical synapses. The presynaptic neuron is a neuron located before the synapse while the postsynaptic neuron is located after a synapse. The presynaptic terminal usually contains synaptic vesicles that have chemical neurotransmitters in them, while the postsynaptic membrane contains specialized receptors.[27] The space in between the synapse is called a synaptic cleft.

Neurotransmitters

Transmission of neurotransmitters takes place when a nerve impulse arrives at the synaptic end bulb of a presynaptic neuron allowing the calcium channels in the bulb to open. When calcium ions flow in, they attract synaptic vesicles to the plasma membrane and help liberate neurotransmitters from the vesicles into the synaptic cleft. This will then be received by the postsynaptic neurons, which serve as integrators by receiving signals, integrating them, and then responding according to the impulses. The release of neurotransmitters will either produce an excitatory transmission or an inhibitory transmission. A chemical transmission is a one-way transmission; hence, nerve impulses must move forward over their pathways.[28]

Since the role of neurotransmitters is to transmit messages through either depolarization or hyperpolarization of the postsynaptic membrane, neurotransmitters therefore play an important role in either the excitation or inhibition of the neurons.

In discussing biological factors as the possible etiology of mood disorder, Kaplan, Sadock, and Grebb write:

> A large number of studies have reported various abnormalities in biogenic amine metabolites . . . in blood, urine, and cerebrospinal fluid (CSF) from patients with mood disorders. The data reported are most consistent with the hypothesis that mood disorders are associated with heterogeneous dysregulations of the biogenic amines.[29]

The biogenic amines often discussed in relation to mood disorders are norepinephrine and serotonin. The level of these neurotransmitters relates to changes in one's mood. Scully states that "deficiencies in the levels of norepinephrine and serotonin have been discovered in depressed patients. . . . Levels of norepinephrine and its metabolites are elevated in mania."[30] In addition to these neurotransmitters, evidence also points to dysregulation of acetylcholine in mood disorder. Similarly, the studies of the biological factors as possible etiology of anxiety point to the role of neurotransmitters such as norepinephrine, serotonin, and gamma-aminobutyric acid (GABA). Bourne points out that the locus ceruleus that contains these neurotransmitters seems to fluctuate more easily and to higher levels of stimulation among people suffering from panic attacks.[31]

Norepinephrine (NE)

The largest and most compact of the nuclei is called the locus ceruleus (LC) and its neurons contain almost 80 percent of all of the

NE in the brain. This nucleus has a very small number of neurons, but they distribute themselves over a very wide area in the brain. The fact that an NE neuron spreads itself over a wide area while at the same time fires in synchrony seems to suggest that this NE pathway does not transmit detailed information but regulates some sort of general function. "Arousal, mood, and the like are obvious possibilities."[32]

The drugs that are commonly associated with norepinephrine are the classic antidepressant drugs such as tricyclic drugs and the monoamine oxidase inhibitors (MAOIs). Tricyclic drugs block the uptake of norepinephrine back into the presynaptic neuron while the MAOIs block the metabolism of norepinephrine. This results in an increment in the level of norepinephrine in the synaptic cleft. However, since three to four weeks are required for the drugs to take effect, the immediate increment of norepinephrine in the synaptic cleft may not be the explanation for the clinical improvement. It is believed that the immediate effect of the antidepressant drugs, which leads to clinical improvement, is the down regulation of the number of postsynaptic beta-adrenergic receptors.[33]

In relation to anxiety, general theory suggests that anxiety disorder is a result of a poorly regulated noradrenergic system resulting in occasional disruptions of activity. Experiments show that by stimulating the locus ceruleus in animals, a fear response is produced. The removal of the locus cerules in animals, on the other hand, blocks the ability to form fear responses.[34]

Serotonin

Serotonin has become the most common biogenic amine neurotransmitter associated with depression, especially in view of the huge effect that SSRIs, such as Prozac, have on the treatment of depression. It is believed that the depletion of serotonin may precipitate depression. It has been found that some suicidal patients have low cerebrospinal fluid concentrations of serotonin metabolites and a low concentration of serotonin uptake sites on platelets. Current serotonin-active antidepressant drugs act primarily by blocking the uptake and the metabolism of serotonin thus increasing the concentration of serotonin in the synaptic cleft.[35]

Dopamine

It has been suggested that the reduction of the level of dopamine activity is related to depression, while an increase in its activity is related to mania. Drugs that reduce dopamine concentrations and diseases such as Parkinson's are associated with depressive symptoms, while drugs that increase dopamine concentrations (tyrosine or amphetamine) reduce depressive symptoms. One theory suggests the dysfunctionality of the dopamine pathway and the hypoactive receptor of dopamine as possible causes of depression.[36]

Amino Acids

Amino acid neurotransmitters are the most abundant neurotransmitters in the brain. These amino acids are glutamate and GABA. Glutamate is the major excitatory amino acid. It is hypothesized that excessive stimulation of glutamate receptors leads to prolonged and excessive intraneuronal concentrations of calcium. This then leads to the activation of many enzymes that are destructive to neuronal integrity. GABA is the major inhibitory amino acid neurotransmitter. GABA receptors produce inhibition when they are activated because they allow chloride to enter the neuron. Chloride ions have a negative charge which increases the negativity inside the cell membrane. Through this process of hyperpolarization of the neurons, the excitatory input is unable to depolarize the cell; its firing is inhibited.[37]

SLEEP PATTERNS AND DEPRESSION

According to T. C. Neylan, 90 percent of patients with major depression experience sleep disruption.[38] This is why the disruption of sleep is an important marker of depression. The sleep laboratory provides perhaps the best predictor for classifying mood disorders. There are basically two types of sleep. These are REM (rapid eye movement) sleep and non-REM sleep. REM sleep takes place later in the night and it is here that we do most of our dreaming. It is also associated with long-term memory. Non-REM sleep is divided into four stages. These four stages are defined by an EEG (electroencephalogram) that records the electrical activity in the brain. The sleep patterns progress from light sleep (stage 1) to deep sleep (stage 4). Stages 3 and 4 are the deepest stages of sleep. Deep sleep occurs during the first half of the night.

The correlation between mood disorders and sleep abnormalities is well established. These abnormalities may be expressed in terms of diminished (difficulty sleeping), excessive (over sleeping), or absent sleep (as in mania).

> One of the most reliable, clinically powerful, but expensive markers of a depressive episode (depressive and bipolar disorder) is the observation that depressed patients go into REM sleep more quickly (sooner than fifty to sixty-five minutes) than normal subjects (called decreased REM latency), have a deficit of slow wave (non-REM, stage 3 and 4) sleep, and have an abnormality in the distribution of dream sleep through the night, with increased REMs in the first half of the night (phase shift). Successful antidepressant treatments normalize these sleep patterns.[39]

It is suggested that for patients who experience decreased REM latency, medication is needed if the treatment is to be effective. The persistence of decreased REM latency during treatment is a good predictor of early relapse among depressed patients.

Sleep patterns have shown to be predictive of how long a person will remain free of depression following drug discontinuation. Patients who recovered from depression, remained in psychotherapy, and experienced enough deep sleep in the first sleep cycle, stayed well five times longer (101 weeks) than patients whose sleep patterns did not normalize. Patients with normal sleep patterns stay depressed-free for an average of two years, with monthly psychotherapy. Without psychotherapy, these patients may relapse as quickly (twenty-three weeks) as patients whose sleep patterns did not normalize. "This means that if the medication makes the patient better, including a normalization of his or her sleep pattern, psychotherapy is necessary to maintain the gains."[40] Those patients whose sleep patterns did not normalize, normally relapse with or without psychotherapy.[41]

BRAIN IMAGING AND DEPRESSION

Most studies indicate decreased blood flow and decreased activity in the frontal areas of the brain of depressed patients. This seems to correspond with patients' complaints of difficulty with clear thinking. A study attempting to measure cerebral blood flow in thirty-one schizophrenic and ten nonpsychotic alcoholic male patients found that "control subjects had relatively higher frontal than posterior blood flow. Patients with schizophrenia had less frontal-posterior blood flow difference; low frontal flow was especially found in patients with symptoms of indifference, inactivity, and autism."[42] Subsequent studies of cerebral blood flow showed decreases in blood flow in the whole right hemisphere in depression and whole left hemisphere in schizophrenia.[43] "Other findings indicate that the fluid-filled spaces in the brain, called ventricles, are larger in patients whose mood disorders have a later onset and are manifested by delusions and hallucinations."[44]

Depression may be affected by other nonpsychiatric factors as well. Pastoral caregivers and counselors need to be aware of the common nonpsychiatric factors that may result in depression such as alcohol dependency,[45] hormonal dysregulation,[46] sleep apnea,[47] and pancreatic cancer.[48]

PSYCHOTROPIC MEDICATIONS

Psychotropic medications, to psychiatrist Robert Hedaya, are based on one principle—the principle of the receptor. "If one understands the receptor, it is relatively easy to understand, in a basic fashion, the hypothesized workings of nearly the entire range of psychiatric medications."[49] The four main structures of the cell related to psychotropic drugs are: (1) the presynaptic vesicles; (2) the synapse (the space between the nerve-cell endings); (3) the postsynaptic receptors; and (4) the reuptake pump.

The presynaptic vesicles are located at the end of the nerve cells. Different nerve cells contain different types of neurotransmitters. When a nerve cell is stimulated, neurotransmitters are released into the synapse. By releasing neurotransmitters into the synapse, a signal is being passed on to another cell. The released neurotransmitters will lock onto a receptor of a receiving cell. The shape of the receptor will be changed, and this change will cause the reactions inside the receiving cell. The remaining neurotransmitters within the synapse are taken back up into the first cell by a reuptake pump. The neurotransmitters that are taken back to the presynaptic vesicles will be dissolved by an enzyme called monoamine oxidase. This enzyme functions to break down neurotransmitters such as serotonin, dopamine, and norepinephrine.[50]

The Mechanism of Antidepressants

The main function of all antidepressants is to block the reuptake pump and they are often known as reuptake inhibitors. The function of the reuptake pump is to get rid of excess neurotransmitters, taking them back to the first nerve cell. When the pump is blocked it increases the amount of neurotransmitters in the synapse. With increased amounts of neurotransmitters in the synapse, more receptors are activated on the surface of the second nerve cell. This results in an increased firing rate. This increase in firing rate becomes an overstimulation for the second nerve cell and eighteen to twenty-one days later it reduces the number of available receptors on its surface. This is when the antidepressants become effective. In fact, all antidepressants cause this down regulation of a particular type of receptor.

The studies of serotonin receptors reveal the same principle. Serotonin receptors (5-HT receptors) can be studied with imipramine (3H IMI), which binds to them with high affinity. It is shown that among depressed patients the binding of 3H IMI is significantly below normal. Studies of suicide victims show a decrease in 3H IMI binding sites and an increase in the density of postsynaptic 5-HT receptors. The increase of postsynaptic receptors seems to indicate a low level of neurotransmitters in the synapse and, hence, a compensatory process results in an increase in postsynaptic receptors. Tricyclic drugs are used as an attempt to increase the serotonin level in the brain.[51]

MAOIs also cause an increase in the amount of neurotransmitters in the synapse, but by a different method. They act by inhibiting the enzyme MAO. The MAO inhibits the enzyme from the process of oxidation and therefore increases the amount of neurotransmitters in the first cell. With the increased amount of neurotransmitters in the first cell, more neurotransmitters are released into the synapse, which will cause the down regulation of receptors in eighteen to twenty-one days.[52]

Administration of Antidepressant Medications

In treating major depressive episodes with antidepressants, the first symptoms "to improve are often poor sleep and appetite patterns. Agitation, anxiety, depressive episodes, and hopelessness are the next symptoms to improve. Other target symptoms include low energy, poor concentration, helplessness, and decreased libido."[53] In the administration of antidepressants, patients need to know that: (1) they will not become addicted to antidepressants because these drugs do not provide immediate gratification; (2) three to four weeks are required for the medications to take effect; (3) side effects will occur (details should be given); and (4) with tricyclic drugs and MAOIs, sleep and appetite will improve first, followed by a sense of returned energy, while the feeling of depression will be the last to be improved.

In the administration of antidepressants, tricyclic drugs are often chosen by physicians because of familiarity and comfort with older drugs. SSRIs are chosen by clinicians whose experience supports the research information on the effectiveness of SSRIs. MAOIs are not often chosen as the first-line drugs because their safe use requires dietary restrictions. The treatment of depression with antidepressants "should be maintained for at least six months or the length of a previous episode, whichever is greater."[54]

Electroconvulsive Therapy (ECT)

An alternative treatment for depression is electroconvulsive therapy (ECT). This form of treatment has been the subject of controversy for many years, yet it is effective in the treatment of depression. Although it is often used as a last resort, it has a good potential in the treatment of dangerously suicidal patients.[55] Two interesting predictors of ECT response are high rigidity with low critical ability or imagination and obsessive personality style.[56] ECT is believed to provide the same effect as antidepressants. It is also a possible alternative for patients who did not show improvement after medication, have no toleration for medications, have severe or psychotic symptoms, and are suicidal or homicidal.[57]

Chapter 3

Overview of Methods of Pastoral Intervention and *Wu Wei*

Pastoral caregivers listen in a certain way to the words of those who are disconsolate, a way that is distinct from other helping professionals. To clergy and other professionals in ministry, despair, suffering, struggle, and adversity are laden with spiritual import, because reflection on the experience of melancholy and spiritual desolation can bring depth and meaning to those who are trying to be faithful to the call of Christ.

Howard Stone[1]

HISTORY OF PASTORAL CARE APPROACHES TO MELANCHOLY

The pastoral awareness of peoples' pain emerging from their inner and social conflicts and the desire to heal has been crucial in the development of the pastoral care movement. Although modern pastoral care theory understands depression as conflict within oneself within the present economic, sociological, and psychological context, in early history, inner conflicts were placed within the context of sin. Sin took away the connection between God and oneself. In the early history of the Christian church, sin was defined as a source of emotional pain expressed as a sense of despair, the loss of hope, the feeling of isolation, alienation from God, and, possibly, depression. The pastoral task was to bring about healing by dealing with sin and alienation.[2]

The Reformation Era

This concern was articulated in classical spiritual literature of a sixteenth-century spiritual leader and poet, St. John of the Cross. His book, the *Dark Night,* expresses the spiritual struggle with the felt absence of God's presence, the fear of losing hold on faith, and sadness resulting from one's persistence in sinfulness. In this experience one seeks to regain and restore the connection with God and yet remains in the sense of disconnection and alienation. "In the dark night of the soul, the sufferer sees or feels little in which to find hope. Hope resides only in the unseen and unfelt."[3]

The struggle within one's soul was also found in the life of Martin Luther. Luther described his sense of despair using the term *Anfechtungen,* which means "to be fought at." This term expresses a sense of despair, doubt, anxiety, and alienation. In the experience of depression, Luther wrote, "I myself was offended more than once, and brought to the depth and abyss of despair, so that I wished that I had never been created a man."[4] One must not despair, was Luther's advice. One must not submit to the sense of despair but must fight back and wrestle with it because despair comes from the devil.[5]

The Post-Reformation Era

During the post-Reformation era, under the influence of John Calvin, personal distress was attributed to an idolatrous heart. Hence, pastoral care involved turning people away from sinful behaviors, an emphasis that deteriorated into legalism. However, David Dickson, a minister from Scotland, tried to journey with those who were in doubt, depression, and temptation. His method was to lead them to repentance and not despair.

In the United States, the Presbyterian pastor Ichabod Spencer sought diligently to lead anxious men and women to repentance. Spencer was very sensitive to individuals in distress, and reflected genuine compassion for their anguish. This compassion probably grew out of his personal experience. He was a man of deep reflection who scrutinized himself constantly and inherited a tendency toward a depressed state of mind. He often complained that he was not fit for the gospel ministry. Spencer eventually suffered a series of nervous breakdowns that affected his work at a large Presbyterian church in Brooklyn. Perhaps it was this very experience that offered him the opportunity to reach out to others in similar circumstances. A story is told of how he helped a woman who had experienced despair for eighteen years discover inner peace. This woman believed that the Holy Spirit had left her because of her sin. Spencer spent many weeks going step by step trying to convince her that God was still with her.

> Spencer called the next day and took up the last item, "reasoning with her, and asking if she thought me right, from step to step." Finally, "her bosom heaved with emotion, and her whole frame seemed agitated with a new kind of life." When Spencer asked her if she still had reason to believe "that her day of grace was past," she began to cry, clasped her hands, and paced the room, exclaiming: "I can be saved! I can be saved!"[6]

Spencer's story reveals the connection between the perception of sin and the experience of despair and how the experience of despair was dealt with through theological discourse. Another individual who made significant contributions to pastoral care during this period was Richard Baxter. Baxter's *Reformed Pastor* (1656) served as a manual that offered guidance on "approaches to various questions of conscience and states of anxiety and depression."[7] According to Baxter, a good counselor should share sorrows, listen well, guard secrets, and pay close attention to disturbed conscience.[8]

Twentieth Century Approaches

A new development in the direction of pastoral care and counseling evolved in the twentieth century. This new direction was prompted by the growth of psychological science. Pastors and theological educators were quick to discern the significance of psychology and psychotherapy for the practice of ministry. This led to the development of clinical training in ministry, starting in the 1920s when a small group of ministers in the United States began to construct a program of professional training that eventually came to be known as Clinical Pastoral Education. The main purpose was not to discover a new method for pastoral ministry but to reshape it. Under the leadership of Richard Cabot and Anton Boisen, training in Clinical Pastoral Education was established.[9]

Again we witness how the shape and form of ministry is influenced by personal, existential experience. The method of "living human documents" proposed by Boisen grew out of his personal struggle with his own tormented soul. He experienced an inordinate amount of guilt relating to sexual fantasy and held a negative perception of himself and his performance as a worker. In his own estimate, he was a failure and hospitalized himself on two occasions as a result of his struggle with mental illness. These experiences were instrumental in the formation of his approaches to treating tormented souls. Clinical pastoral education, therefore, was a study of sin and salvation.

> [H]e believed that the key to understanding the self lay in its pathological eruptions. No sharp line divided the insane from the normal. Schizophrenic torment offered a clearer insight into the human personality than did any process of biological growth in tissues and cells.[10]

This short review of the development of pastoral care and counseling shows the centrality of the soul in the healing process. The place of healing seems to be located in the reconciliation of the inner self. To reconcile presupposes conflicts. This resonates with the theme of this dissertation that although our understanding and experience of conflicts may differ due to the historical, economic, and political contexts of each period, the pastoral aim remains constant. Pastoral responsibility aims at bringing inner reconciliation to the soul.

CURRENT PASTORAL CARE APPROACHES TO DEPRESSION

A good place to start the review of literature dealing with current practical approaches for pastoral caregivers is the article "Depression," by Howard Stone. This article provides a comprehensive guide for ministers and pastoral caregivers in helping depressed individuals.[11] Stone instructs pastoral caregivers and ministers to restrict their help to those suffering from mild and moderate depression[12] and to refer severely depressed individuals to mental health professionals. Mild depression refers to occasional sad or blue feelings that fluctuate considerably. Moderate depression refers to a more persistent feeling of sadness and lack of interest that does not go away easily.

Any relief is often temporary and treatment often requires a longer period than that of mild depression. Severe depression involves a feeling of complete hopelessness, accompanied by physical symptoms that immobilize a person.

The first meeting should consist of taking a history, establishing a relationship, assessing the severity of depressed feelings, and allowing the person to express his or her feelings and the existing problems. At this point a clear distinction must be made between grief and depression, because treatment for grief differs from that of depression. While ministering to people in grief calls for continuing support and the process of reconnection, depressed individuals need fundamental restructuring of the self.

Once it is clear that the individual is experiencing depression (a number of assessment tools may be used),[13] pastoral caregivers and pastors need to look into the immediate difficulties; assess the strength (skills, abilities, and resources that may have been forgotten or devalued); decide whether the symptoms are primarily behavioral, physiological, cognitive, or affective; and make a decision on the approach to use. Pastoral caregivers and ministers may find, through the process of assessment, that one visit that encourages expression of feelings and looking into the immediate problems may be sufficient. If an individual needs more than one visit but is not depressed enough to require the use of psychotropic medications, ministers can provide continual sustenance through visitation. During these visits, ministers can encourage the depressed to discuss his or her difficulties and resources, enhancing self-esteem, and empowering the depressed person. Stone proposes other approaches that may require a longer period of time. These different approaches are affective treatment,[14] behavioral therapy, physiological intervention,[15] and cognitive therapy.

In *Depression and Hope* (1998), Stone continues by raising the question of the relationship between the experience of depression and faith in Christian churches and points out that by placing emphasis on the past and on the negative events experienced by depressed individuals, psychotherapy may nurture negativity instead of providing healing. He thus emphasizes the place of hope in the healing ministry of pastoral caregivers and counselors. Depressed people focus on the negative and experience the inability to recall the peaceful and happy moments of their lives. Pastors need to slowly bring to mind these

positive events. This can be achieved through reframing. Reframing
is not an attempt at arguing the clients out of their illogical view-
points, but is entering into the world and reality of depressed people
and finding within that experience a gap that has been overlooked.
Together they reflect on this gap. "The space widens, new light shines
on the situation, and change becomes possible."[16] *Depression and
Hope* offers an overview of the problem of depression and also discusses a number of approaches that can be used by pastoral counselors. Of special interest to me is Stone's usage of spiritual direction,
since it can be readily employed by pastoral caregivers.[17]

Cognitive reframing is widely used because of its effectiveness.
Stone's use of reframing is particularly helpful in light of the principle
of *wu wei* in that it does not seek to argue the illogical viewpoint and at
the same time it encourages pastoral caregivers to enter the reality of
depressed individuals. In so doing, depressed individuals are not pres-
sured to get rid of their negativity. However, instead of searching for a
gap within their experience, it may be helpful to take a more active role
in embracing the negativity itself. Further, there are times when depressed individuals feel totally paralyzed by the symptoms of depression. During this period, they may not want to do anything. Perhaps at
this point, the principle of *wu wei* (non-trying) may be utilized and the
process of embracing and emptying may be welcomed by depressed
individuals.

Use of Biblical Passages

Roy W. Fairchild, in his article "Sadness and Depression,"[18] suggests the use of community and biblical images. He proposes different biblical passages that are helpful in dealing with the emerging
themes of negative views of one's future, guilt, anger, paralysis of
will, and unfinished mourning among depressed individuals. Examples given are the Psalms of lament (Psalms 6, 22, 28, 31, 51, 63, 69),
that will provide "homes" for those who feel alone in their struggle;
the book of Job; or New Testament passages that acknowledge the
acceptability of honest anger (Matthew 23: 23-26; John 2:13-17). I
strongly agree that community and support are important sources of
strength for people experiencing depression. The use of biblical passages, too, can be healing, since they help to locate the struggle

within the context of depressed individuals' faith. Perhaps the use of biblical passages dealing with the call to emptiness can enhance the application of the principle of *wu wei.* The crucial question is how these passages are being interpreted. If these passages are used for the purpose of identification, then perhaps it can bring relief to depressed individuals. But if they are used to show that through faith these individuals were able to overcome their distress, then guilt would be aggravated and the gap between the "is" and the "ought" increased.

In "Pastoral Counseling Dealing with Depression," Richard Dayringer and Myron C. Madden discuss the need to journey with an individual who is experiencing emptiness. This is to be with the person in the grief process and, at the same time, to bring to awareness possibilities for the future. In journeying with depressed individuals, it is important to provide affirmation. "People want affirmation. They need affirmation; they need love, they need acceptance."[19] I like this approach because not only does it encourage pastoral caregivers to walk with depressed people in their struggle with negativity, but it provides affirmation along the way as well. Validating people's experience helps to shift attention away from themselves and thus reduces the power of negation.

Three Pastoral Functions in Treating Depression

Pastoral counselor Binford W. Gilbert, in his book *The Pastoral Care of Depression: A Guidebook,* proposes three pastoral functions. First, the pastor must seek to transform victimhood among depressed individuals. Using biblical teachings, depressed individuals need to know that they are still in control of their destiny and that God has given them the power to reclaim their future. Second, the pastor needs to encourage depressed individuals who seek isolation and withdrawal to learn to take risks just as Jesus did when he encouraged "[h]is disciples to get out of the boat and try something new."[20] The third pastoral role is to support them through the use of logotherapy. Pastors are trained in theological reflection that can be a main source of meaning for individuals experiencing meaninglessness in life.[21]

In my estimate, these three functions seem to promote greater self-evaluation and encourage self-regulation. Relief occurs when self-regulation is able to close the gap between the "is" and the "ought" brought about through self-evaluation. If this "ought" is redefined in a way that does not take away the validity of the experience of negativity, this approach can be very helpful. Otherwise it can widen the gap and trap depressed individuals in a downward spiral.

The one common factor that I find helpful among these approaches is the use of cognitive reframing through biblical passages. The benefit of using biblical images in the treatment of depression is affirmed in a study by Rebecca Propst, who found that the usage of religious images is more effective in altering dysfunctional self-statements in comparison to nonreligious images.[22] An example of this, suggests pastoral theologian Susan J. Dunlap, is how one can help depressed women deal with their anger by pointing to the biblical God who was angry for righteousness's sake.[23] Or how pastors can use the humanity of Jesus (he experienced hunger, thirst, and loneliness) to help depressed individuals deal with "parent-child" scripts within them.[24]

FEMINIST PASTORAL CARE

It is important at this point to examine feminist pastoral care and counseling approaches since more women than men are being diagnosed with depression. Why is this so? Perhaps other variables need to be considered. According to feminist pastoral theologians, social context plays an important role in affecting the high rate of depression among women. This social context refers to patriarchal attitudes and responses to gender roles.

In her book *Counseling Depressed Women* (1997), Susan Dunlap utilizes the work of Michel Foucault, a French poststructuralist philosopher, in her analysis of the social context that many argue fosters a depressive tendency among women. Foucault argues that standards and definitions are formed by people in power. These standards and definitions are transmitted to the level of day-to-day operation through the media. "I would like to suggest that there exists a misogynist web of institutions, practices, language, and psyches, which I will call 'truth-of-woman' discourse, that fosters depression among women."[25] This "truth-of-woman" discourse includes the stereotype of "good woman" as passive, dependent, helpless, and "bad woman" as strong, sexual, and independent. She proposes the use of cognitive therapy in dealing with distorted constructs of the meaning of "woman" in the areas of self, relationship, bodies, anger, and hope. In using cognitive therapy she urges pastoral caregivers to recognize (1) the cultural beliefs and assumptions about women; (2) the dynamics of inter-relatedness of economy, culture, institutions, language, rituals, and symbols that are being internalized by people within the culture; (3) the potency of the dominant cultural discourse that perpetuates dysfunctional beliefs and interpretations; and (4) the awareness that our judgment of what appears to be dysfunctional and irrational may be located within our own subculture.[26]

In her article "Women's Depression: Lives at Risk," Christie Cozad Neuger argues for a feminist model to conceptualize the problem of depression.[27] Neuger suggests that the high rate of depression among women is the result of the internalization process of misogyny among women living in a patriarchal society. "Feminist approaches," says Neuger, "see depression primarily as an attempted adaptive reaction to a destructive culture."[28] This destructive culture refers to women suffering from different forms of abuse, such as the 50 percent of women who experience violence in their marriages, the two to six million women who are battered annually in the United States, the 750,000 women who are raped yearly in the United States, and women who compose two-thirds of the world's poor adults. She urges pastoral caregivers to take cultural contexts seriously when caring for women who are depressed and suggests corrective action that includes the following steps: (1) encouraging women to tell their stories; (2) validating women's experience; (3) associating with other women; (4) drawing boundaries while learning to recognize interdependency; and (5) negotiating new behavior with the support of counselors.

Both Dunlap and Neuger's suggestions about how one can help women suffering from depression address the core theological and philosophical issues that have direct impacts on women, such as the patriarchal understanding of God and the values place on feminine qualities. This need to address theological and philosophical issues is also an important part of the principle of *wu wei*. What is the connection, one may ask, since feminists recognize the need to take an active role in social reform but the principle of *wu wei* only asks that one sits and do nothing? Is not non-doing a contributing factor to the depressive symptoms among women? I believe that the art of *wu wei* is the art of self-definition that refuses to allow the self to be defined by social constructs. When one can learn not to try to prove or affirm, this very act of non-trying affirms the existential reality of womanhood as is.

Rumination

A pastoral care approach that approaches the theory of self-regulatory perseveration is suggested by Mary Louise Bringle, professor of religious studies at St. Andrews Presbyterian College. In her article, "'I Just Can't Stop Thinking About It': Depression, Rumination, and Forgiveness," she uses the concept of rumination in her understanding of depressive symptoms. Rumination is a process of continuous focusing on the negativity, the inability to stop thinking about issues that are disturbing. The concept of rumination as a coping method of depressed individuals is proposed by Susan Nolen-Hoeksema in her studies of gender differences.[29] To silence this cycle, Bringle suggests the use of support through church community, cognitive therapy in combating hurtful thoughts, and forgiveness. Forgiveness means to see others as a child of God and to recognize weaknesses within ourselves as well. Forgiveness is letting go of one's point of view and entering that of God's.[30] These approaches recognize the vicious cycle experienced by depressed individuals and encourage the art of letting go, which is similar which is similar to the teachings of Lao Tzu and Chuang Tzu on the need to empty oneself.

In her article "Soul-Dye and Salt: Integrating Spiritual and Medical Understandings of Depression," Bringle introduces concepts that are also closely related to the principle of *wu wei.* The term "nevertheless" reflects the tempo of life. Life has its rhythm. Sadness may be a part of it but not all. This concept is contrary to the absolutizing tendency whereby "the way things are right now is the way they are going to be forever and ever."[31] "The gift of a dark sun" is another concept. The darkness of the sun represents the light that comes through the experience of depression. "As spiritual directors and as spiritual disciples, we need to be reminded of this final pastoral teaching, that depression can be a gift."[32]

Wu Wei *and Pastoral Care*

Where is the place of *wu wei* among these various pastoral care and counseling approaches? As I stated earlier, the history of the development of pastoral care and counseling recognizes the soul as the central focus of pastoral ministry. At the conceptual level, it aims at the inner reconciliation of the self. Recent approaches, likewise, attempt to achieve inner reconciliation of the self through cognitive, behavioral, and interpersonal interventions using biblical images and language. The difference between these recent approaches and previous attempts lies in the present historical context where psychological theories have heightened awareness of the self. This context forms the new reality through which one assesses oneself and others. The self that must be reconciled is the self that must come to define itself through this awareness. In this awareness, the language has changed. Instead of sin, we have the libido. Instead of mutual dependency, we speak of codependency. This is the reality that the self must be reconciled to in dealing with depression. This is also where *wu wei* differs from these approaches. While *wu wei* may employ, to some extent, cognitive and behavioral interventions, it questions the philosophical and theological basis of this definition of the self. It questions the interpretation of reality upon which our culture arrives at the meaning of "healthy self." Hence, when the soul speaks through depression of the need to find inner reconciliation, *wu wei* does not seek to reconcile the self to its perception of reality but challenges the theology that forms the basis of this perception.

Having said that, I wish to also comment that Dunlap's approach to the problem of depression also addresses the social reality from which the meaning of womanhood is defined. She does not ask women to seek reconciliation to this social reality but to see the role of pastoral care as a critique of social reality.

Chapter 4

Negativity and Trying

Fill your bowl to the brim and it will spill. Keep sharpening your knife and it will blunt. Chase after money and security and your heart will never unclench. Care about people's approval and you will be their prisoner. Do your work, then step back, the only path to serenity.

Lao Tzu[1]

Most individuals with depression have very little self-esteem and experience a lack of meaning or purpose in life. This lack of purpose is described by David Rosen, a Jungian analyst, as "meaninglessness and inner emptiness"[2] which, argue Gotlib and Hammen, is the result of one's "appraisal of the meaning of the event as signaling loss of self-worth."[3] This experience leads one to try to affirm oneself through the process of self-evaluation. This process of self-evaluation leads one to try to affirm oneself through self-regulation. In so doing, one gets caught in the cycle of self-preservation because one's worth is attached to one's ability to reduce discrepancy. This theory, by Pyszczynski and Greenberg, proposes that depression may not be the result of the individual giving up on goals, but rather, the inability to give up on unobtainable goals when it is adaptive to do so.[4]

SELF-REGULATORY PERSEVERATION THEORY

In the late 1970s, Pyszczynski and Greenberg noticed a relationship between depression and self-awareness. They hypothesized that self-awareness is high among depressed individuals. This resulted in many studies and experiments. They came to believe that depressed individuals are highly self-focused and have a tendency to be absorbed within themselves. Further, these individuals engage in self-focus after failure more than self-focus after success. The questions raised are: Why are they highly self-focused? and Why do they focus on themselves after failure instead of after success? Depression, to Pyszczynski and Greenberg, is the consequence of "perseverated efforts" to regain a lost object that cannot be reclaimed. [5] Perseveration takes place when a person has lost the sense of self-worth while at the same time lacks an alternative source to regain this self-worth. This leads to a high level of self-focus that according to Pyszczynski and Greenberg, maximizes the symptoms of depression. This negative affect includes self-blame, disparagement, and the lack of motivation which, in turn, reinforces negative self-image and depressive self-focusing style. This whole process of perseveration perpetuates the depressed state.

What we see here is the self getting trapped within a cycle. It starts with the external or internal stimuli that cause the individual to focus on the self. This stimuli causes the awareness of discrepancy, the awareness that "I am not what I ought to be." This leads the person into the process of self-evaluation. The person compares oneself with one's own standards and thus sees oneself as falling short of what one ought to be. This comparison intensifies affects and encourages self-blame. The intensified affects activate the self-regulatory system. This self-regulatory system has the function of closing the gap. "Only by engaging a self-regulatory cycle can one be certain that one is, indeed, valuable. Only by comparing oneself with standards can shortcomings in oneself be corrected." [6]

In this attempt, when the goal becomes unattainable, the self keeps persisting because self-esteem is essential for survival. Self-esteem is an essential factor if one is to survive as a human being within the society. Self-esteem allows the individual to hold on to self in the face of existential despair, in the face of death and dying. Self-esteem makes possible the opportunity of remaining within the recognition that this being is being toward death. Self-esteem provides a buffer against the anxiety of death. This persistence in the self-regulatory process leads to depression. Once one experiences depression, the cycle continues. The continuation of this cycle results in the symptoms of depression.

DEPRESSION AND NEGATIVITY

What is this experience of negativity? The experience of negativity refers to the sense of despair, feeling of hopelessness, negative self-perception and self-evaluation, and the tendency to focus on the negative, complicated by irrationality. Occasionally, a former patient of mine, who has gone through episodes of depression, would call me and say, "I still experience a lot of negative thoughts. I keep analyzing everything, and I see everything in the negative." The experience of negativity is one of the most disturbing factors in depression. It is important because it is one of the main factors that contributes to the maintenance of the symptoms of depression.[7] It affects many areas of life, such as interpersonal relations, memory recall, interpretation, guilt, and self-perception.

Existential Description

A male custodian described his experience with depression:

> I've referred to it as a dark storm at sea. The sea would, like, relate to the insecurity. You're going to sink. You're going to lose yourself, your life, your everything, and then sink to death. I guess, maybe the sea is death. And the dark storm is, I think, hopelessness. The sea is below you. There is a storm above you. It's a dark storm between your ears. That's how I see it . . . mean it's doom, it's hopelessness, down the water is death, and up is just a dark storm that you want to get away from, but can't. . . . That's why the sense of doom. And that causes a paralysis, you know. . . . The sense of doom actually paralyzes you. . . . It incapacitates you.[8]

The negativity of depression has been expressed in different words and phrases. According to Karp, many of his subjects arrived at very similar metaphors in describing depression. These are "drowning, suffocating, descending into a bottomless pit, or being in a lightless tunnel."[9] Novelist William Styron's experience with depression evoked a line from Baudelaire, "I have felt the wind of the wing of madness."[10] Susan Dunlap, a pastoral counselor, uses the term "brain pain" to describe the experience of depression. In explaining this term she writes, "For many who have been depressed, not only is the face of God eclipsed, but their own souls are in eclipse. Faith dies, hope withers, love is impossible. The sense of isolation and self-loathing is overwhelming."[11] Thomas Moore employs the terms "void" and "grayness."[12]

Research

The concept of negativity in depression is the main focus in cognitive therapy.[13] In *Cognitive Theory and the Emotional Disorders,* Aaron Beck suggests three components of depression: negative automatic thoughts (negative view of the self, experiences, and the future), systematic logical errors, and depressogenic schemata.[14] Numerous studies have been conducted to prove these three cognitive dysfunctional aspects of depression. Although the results may not fully correspond to Beck's hypothesis, "there is little question that currently depressed persons differ from nondepressed individuals with respect to their cognitive functioning."[15]

In an attempt to prove Beck's hypothesis that depressed individuals exhibit depressogenic schemata, a number of researchers presented subjects with positive, neutral, and negative stimuli. The subjects were then asked to recall the number of positive and negative stimuli. Some researchers have found that depressed individuals tend to underestimate positive reinforcement.[16] Lora Lee Sloan's research presented a prose passage with half of the passages containing negative affective valence and another half of neutral affective valence to seventy undergraduate students. These students completed the Beck Depression Inventory (BDI) and the Geriatric Depression Scale (GDS) prior to the process. Individuals scoring more than ten in the BDI and eleven on the GDS were classified as depressed. "Prose passage recall analyses indicated that depressed subjects remembered more idea units from negative passages than neutral passages and exhibited superior recall to nondepressed subjects for negative word lists."[17] In reviewing a number of studies, Gotlib and Hammen conclude, "It appears, therefore, that consistent with Beck's schema theory . . . depressed persons demonstrate an attentional bias toward negative stimuli."[18]

Regarding negative self-perception, a number of studies have found correlation between low self-concept and depression, and that depressed individuals evaluate their role-playing task more negatively than their nondepressed counterparts.[19] Others have found that depressed individuals rate their laboratory task performances more negatively than nondepressed individuals.[20] Depressed individuals see themselves as inferior in areas such as intelligence and social status.[21] They have low self-esteem and engage in self-focus after failure.[22] They "endorse more depression-related negative adjectives as self-descriptive than do either normal or anxious subjects."[23]

Another important characteristic of cognitive impairment among depressed individuals is systematic logical error, or irrational thinking. Beck described this characteristic as, "The depressed patient shows certain patterns of illogical thought. The systematic errors, leading to distortions of reality, include arbitrary interpretation, selective abstraction, overgeneralization, exaggeration, and incorrect labeling."[24]

Studies based on a questionnaire designed to measure negative cognitive distortion (negative view of the world, self, and the future) such as the Cognitive Biases Questionnaire,[25] the Automatic Thoughts Questionnaire,[26] and the Cognition Checklist,[27] have shown that depressed individuals have the tendency toward negative cognitive distortion.

How does this focus on the negativity of interpretation and self-perception affect other areas of life? Psychiatrist Carol Anderson and family therapists Sona Dimidjian and Apryl Miller write, "as they [depressed individuals] selectively attend to negative events and feelings, their sensitivity to criticism, feelings of worthlessness, and compromised self-esteem make it difficult for them to accept positive feedback and support."[28] This leads us to the question of the relationship between negativity and interpersonal relations.

Negativity and Interpersonal Relations

How does this negativity affect interpersonal relations? The tendency to interpret events in a negative way and to view oneself negatively often leads to social impairment. When individuals view themselves negatively, they tend to think that they are inferior to others. For this reason, there is a general expectation that others will treat them poorly.[29] James C. Coyne studied social interactions of depressed individuals by examining the reactions of female undergraduate students to telephone conversations with depressed and nondepressed female psychiatric outpatients. He found that subjects reported feeling significantly more depressed and hostile after their interactions with depressed patients than with nondepressed patients.[30] Reflecting on this research, Gotlib and Hammen write:

> These results are consistent with the hypothesis that behavior of depressed persons is aversive and capable of inducing negative affect in others. Equally important is the finding that the behavior of the depressed patients also resulted in other people rejecting opportunities for further interaction, a situation that clearly restricts the interpersonal contact available to the depressed person.[31]

In marital relations, the focus on the negative is not often viewed by spouses as a consequence of depression, but rather as a reflection of the individual's feeling toward marital and family relationship.[32] Not interpreting the focus on the negative as a symptom of depression often results in the disruption of communication and in marital conflicts.

It is, therefore, not surprising to learn that depressed individuals judge themselves to be less socially competent than nondepressed individuals. For this reason, negativity has a great impact on social interaction.[33] Karp writes, "depressive feelings make interaction arduous and sometimes the need to withdraw from others overrides the realization that self-isolation will only deepen one's anguish."[34] A depressed female graduate student describes the process:

> It's this real catch-22 because you feel bad and you feel that if you see your friends you're going to make them feel bad too, or you're not going to have a good time. Or you're just going to complain. You're going to whine. So then you want to stay by yourself, but if you stay by yourself it just gets worse and worse and worse.[35]

Summary

Numerous other studies exist on the relationship between negativity and depression, but for the purpose of this dissertation we can reasonably conclude that negativity causes overwhelming pain to individuals in depression. This pain affects one's interpretation of events in life, one's relationship with others, and one's view of oneself. Reflecting on this negativity of depression and self-evaluation, Lynn Rehm and Mary Naus write:

> Depressed persons make negative evaluations of their perfor-
> mance. Depressed persons are more likely to accept negative in-
> formation as true about themselves. Their past, present, and
> future behavior is judged as more negative and less positive
> though perception and prediction of performance may be accu-
> rate and normal. Depressed persons make more frequent nega-
> tive self-evaluations, set stringent standards for themselves, are
> more likely to punish substandard behavior, and less likely to re-
> ward adequate performance. Depressed persons attend more to
> negative information about themselves.[36]

This negativity produces a sense of helplessness, hopelessness, and meaninglessness. One becomes helpless because the focus on negativity together with other physical symptoms such as fatigue and agitation paralyze oneself. The experience of helplessness suggests inability to take control over one's life. This lack of control leads to a feeling of hopelessness because one is unable to produce the desired effect for the future. An unemployed disabled female writes, "You don't have any control (over) your thinking or how despairing you feel or how morose you start feeling. It just takes off."[37]

This lack of control is compounded by the tendency toward negative recollection. The inability to remember any positive aspect of oneself reminds us of the experience of William Styron after winning the del Duca prize. "I was persuaded that I could not be worthy of the prize, that I was in fact not worthy of any of the recognition that had come my way in the past few years."[38] When there is no past and no future, life becomes meaningless. One plunges into the abyss. Having described the experience of negativity, the question is, what is the mechanism of negativity that has the power to negate and trap depressed individuals in its cycle? The next section will explore the first part of this mechanism. Negativity leads to the process of self-evaluation.

NEGATIVITY AND SELF-EVALUATION

The experience of negativity leads one to question oneself. What is my worth? This self-doubt forms the basis of the quest for one's iden-tity. To arrive at an identity implies criteria whereby one can evaluate oneself. This section explores the relationship between negativity and self-evaluation, the first argument of this chapter, which states that the experience of negativity leads one to try to affirm oneself through the process of self-evaluation. To accomplish this, I first explore the relationship between the quest for identity and depression and how this quest for self-affirmation leads to self-evaluation.

Negativity and the Quest for Identity

Negativity has a way of bringing to consciousness questions regarding one's identity. In his studies, based on interviews of fifty clinically depressed individuals, Karp observed that the question of identity formation is central to the struggle with the negativity of depression. A depressed person is "caught up with assessing self, redefining self, reinterpreting past selves, and attempting to construct a future self that will 'work' better."[39] I remember asking a friend who was experiencing depression what occupies her thought most of the time. Her reply was, "Am I going to amount to anything at all?" Negativity makes one wonder about oneself because, in focusing on the negative aspects of the self, the questions naturally emerge: "Why am I a failure? If I am a failure, is there any meaning at all in being me?" "I keep asking myself," said a depressed friend, "what is the meaning of life if you laugh with your friends for a while and spend the rest of the time feeling so unhappy?"

Underlying this quest for identity is the question of self-worth. Before this self can assess its worth, it has to go through an evaluative process, comparing itself to standards. In an attempt to know if one is a good worker, a standard must be established whereby one can decide the meaning of "good worker" and "bad worker." To know one's worth presupposes knowledge of the meaning of worthlessness. Consequently, the obsessive quest for the worth of the self, initiated by feelings of negativity, leads to the process of self-evaluation. In commenting on this process, pastoral counselor Gilbert states, "Depressives see themselves as failures because they do not, or did not, live up to expectations of themselves or those placed by an internal mother image that can never be satisfied."[40] This process of self-evaluation presupposes a standard or criteria whereby one may judge oneself. Perhaps Hammen has this in mind when he writes:

Depression is the unique outcome of beliefs in the unworthiness, inadequacy, and depletion of the self. That is, evaluations about one's worth and one's efficacy seem particularly likely to be associated with affect. Moreover ... we expect that individuals may differ in the kinds of circumstances or objects that their feelings of self-evaluation and efficacy become attached to. Thus, it has been speculated that two domains of functioning, such as work/achievement or interpersonal relationships, may have different meanings to individuals in terms of how central these domains are to the person's sense of self.[41]

Self-Affirmation and Self-Evaluation

According to Chuang Tzu, we seek self-affirmation through the process of self-evaluation. In expressing Chuang Tzu's thought, Kuang-ming Wu writes, "one strains at attaining cultural values, and one strains oneself to deformity; one strives at fulfilling values, and is plagued with internal strife."[42] How does one strain oneself to deformity? The answer is: "Seeing the webbed toes and the sixth finger to be contrary to 'what ought to be,' the reflexive self undertakes corrective measures, only to result in an unwitting deformation of the empirical self."[43] Are these just philosophical words that can mean anything or can Chuang Tzu's analysis be substantiated? I suggest that social science has produced sufficient evidence to show the connection between self-affirmation and self-evaluation. This connection is prominent in the self-focus theory of Duval and Wicklund that has been applied to the problem of depression by Pyszczynski and Greenberg.

Self-Focus and Self-Evaluation

According to Pyszczynski and Greenberg, the intellectual root of this theory can be traced to the symbolic interactionist perspectives of George Herbert Mead and the cognitive developmental psychology of Jean Piaget.[44] Mead believes that the development of self-consciousness is the result of one's attempt at understanding oneself through others' point of view. In this process, one leaves oneself experientially and looks at oneself from the perspectives of other persons.[45] Piaget views the development of self-consciousness as an attempt at logical understanding. Logic involves verification, which requires the ability to step back and look at oneself from a more objective point of view.[46] Understanding of the effects of self-focused attention has been further developed by Duval and Wicklund. Carver and Scheier made use of the basic concepts by Duval and Wicklund and combined them with control theory of self-regulation.

Duval and Wicklund's theory is called "objective self-awareness." According to this theory, conscious awareness can be focused either internally on the self or externally on the environment. Therefore, there are basically two types of attentional focus: objective self-awareness and subjective self-awareness. Objective self-awareness refers to the state of self-focused attention, which "involves taking the self as an object."[47] Here consciousness does not become conscious of objects outside of itself, but the self becomes the object of consciousness. When in this state "consciousness is focused exclusively on the self and consequently the individual attends to his conscious state, his personal history, his body, or any other personal aspects of himself."[48]

Subjective self-awareness, on the other hand, refers to the state of being externally focused. The consciousness of the subject "is directed toward external objects."[49] Within this state, individuals are aware of the external events but not of themselves. They do not become the object of consciousness. They become conscious of the object outside of them. Therefore they are able to experience external events directly without being conscious of themselves in this process.

 According to this theory, objective self-awareness is instigated by external stimuli that draw attention to the self. "Focusing attention on the self inevitably leads to comparison of one's current state with one's standards."[50] The dimension to be evaluated depends on the aspect of the self that is of importance at the time of self-consciousness. If morality becomes the context of the self-focused attention, the self will evaluate the moral ethical aspects of oneself. For example, if while trying to lie to my wife about my weight I see myself in a mirror, the reflection of myself (self-focused attention) will make me think twice about lying and my conscience will be activated. There are affective and motivational consequences to this comparison. Because standards are usually set at a level that is higher than what people can normally achieve, self-focus would produce negative affect. This negative affect will serve to motivate individuals to try harder to reduce the gap. Whether self-focused attention will produce positive or negative results depends on whether an individual can or cannot achieve the standards. If, for example, after resisting my craving for chocolate ice cream and fried chicken for a month I still miss my mark by four pounds, I will continue the focus on myself and experience negative affect and self-blame. Duval and Wicklund further suggest that if one is unable to achieve the desired state, one will escape or avoid self-focus as a way of reducing negative affect.[51]

Pyszczynski and Greenberg agree with the general approach of Duval and Wicklund, but add that self-focus is not necessarily instigated only by external stimuli. Internal stimuli as well can lead to self-focus attention. Internal stimuli here may refer to an internal recognition that one is not what one ought to be. This internal awareness of one's discrepancy is common among depressed individuals. An inordinate sense of guilt among depressed individuals illustrates this internal awareness that triggers the process of self-evaluation.

Research

Depressed individuals have been found, by a number of studies, to engage in an emotion-focused coping method.[52] This is reflected in an experiment by Ingram and Smith using a sentence completion scale as a means of measuring self-focused attention. They found that depressed individuals were more self-focused than nondepressed individuals.[53] Studies have also investigated the theory that self-awareness activates an evaluative process that makes one compare oneself to the standard of whatever was important to the individual at the moment.[54] Wicklund and Duval conducted research that indirectly supports this theory. In their studies they have found that when subjects were asked to copy drawings while being exposed to a mirror, they tended to inspect their work more frequently.[55] Scheier and Carver have also found that a high level of public self-consciousness is closely related to the tendency to engage in social comparison in the process of self-evaluation. They therefore conclude that self-focused attention increases the search for standards necessary for one to evaluate oneself. "Hence, the major outcome of increased self-focus is a greater correspondence between behavior and behavioral standards." [56]

In stating the connection between self-affirmation and self-evaluation, it is appropriate to close with a statement from Pyszczynski and Greenberg:

> According to self-awareness theories, focusing attention on oneself leads to the instigation of a self-evaluative process by which one's present state on a currently salient dimension is compared with whatever standard for that dimension is most salient at the time.[57]

What happens, then, when depressed individuals seek self-affirmation through self-evaluation? The next section will explore the relationship between self-evaluation and self-regulation, which is the second step in the mechanism of negativity.

SELF-EVALUATION AND SELF-REGULATION

In the previous section, I explained how self-focused attention leads to self-evaluation. In this section I will explore the connection between self-evaluation and self-regulation. Reflecting on Chuang Tzu's understanding of self-evaluation and self-regulation, Kuang-ming Wu writes,

> The fault lies in setting up a standard of what one ought to be. The standard induces antagonism between the clever and the stupid, the righteous and the wicked, and the rich and the poor, in a word, the successful people and those who "did not make it." Such discrimination prostitutes people into "trying" and "laboring" to reach the dangled prize of excellence, which now enslaves them.[58]

In psychological terms, how does this take place?

Self-Regulation

According to Pyszczynski and Greenberg, people self-focus when their attention is directed inward. This leads to the process of comparison. If a discrepancy is detected, the self-regulatory process will be intensified and thus increasing the focus on self.[59]

Carver and Scheier explain the movement from self-evaluation to self-regulation in their control theory approach to self-regulation, which is an expansion of Duval and Wicklund's objective self-awareness. In this theory, Carver and Scheier added the general control theory of self-regulation in order to explain how self-focus leads to self-regulation. Self-regulation here refers to the attempt of the self to close the gap between the "is" and the "ought-to-be." The self-regulates itself in an attempt to reduce the discrepancy. Hence, while self-focused attention involves comparing current aspects of self with a standard and noting any discrepancy, the perceived discrepancy will engage an individual with mechanisms that function to reduce discrepancies.[60] While in this process, the individual finds himself or herself shifting between engaging in a discrepancy-reducing behavior and comparisons with standards. This movement will continue until the individual is able to reduce the discrepancy or realize that successful discrepancy reduction is not possible.[61]

The attempt to self-regulate, according to this theory, will come to a place where the self recognizes that one has successfully reduced the discrepancy or else that this process is unlikely to happen. When this takes place, a person will exit the self-regulatory cycle. Once exited, the level of self-focus decreases.

In reviewing a number of studies of self-awareness, Pyszczynski and Greenberg point out a number of adaptive values of self-focused attention. Self-focus leads to self-regulation as an attempt to reduce discrepancies in that it increases the internality of individuals' causal attributions. Therefore it increases one's desire to take responsibility for oneself. It also increases the accuracy of self-reports and decreases the effectiveness of placebo manipulation. Finally, when one is self-focused, one thinks of oneself in evaluative terms. Thinking in evaluative terms often results in increased affect as a result of awareness of the discrepancy. If emotion plays an important role in motivating future behavior, we can conclude that the intensified affect will intensify the need to engage in discrepancy-reducing behavior.[62]

Research

Sufficient evidence supports the hypothesis that self-focused attention encourages self-regulation, which is an attempt of the self to reduce discrepancy. Ed Diener and Thomas K. Srull's study supports this hypothesis. In their study, Diener and Srull selected twenty-four male and twenty-four female introductory psychology students for the experiment. In this experiment, each student was supposed to read twelve slides. Each slide contained a large number of dots. They were supposed to guess the number of dots on each slide. After guessing, they were asked to estimate how successful they were in guessing the number of dots. When they had finished estimating, the examiner revealed the answers, which had been manipulated, by comparing the participants' answers with their performance level, self-standard (participants' criteria in determining successful guessing), and social standard. After the examiner revealed answers that were manipulated, each subject was asked to pick a number of marbles as rewards for his or her performance. Under the self-aware condition, the level of self-awareness was manipulated by having the subject's image projected on a television screen. The results showed that students who performed higher than their own standard but not that of their social standard rewarded themselves much higher in the non-self-aware condition than in the self-aware condition. On the other hand, students rewarded themselves more highly when they performed better than the social standard in the non-self-aware condition. Under the self-aware condition they did not reward themselves even when they performed higher than their self-standard. The study concludes that high self-awareness leads to greater conformity with social norms.[63] It also encourages moral behavior.

In the study of the relationship between self-awareness and transgression in children, 363 Halloween trick-or-treaters were instructed to take only one piece of candy. In the self-aware group, each child was also asked to state his or her name and address and a mirror was placed behind the candy bowl. The result showed the transgression rate to be lower in the self-aware group in comparison to the anonymous group.[64]

A study by Frederick X. Gibbons on sexual standards and reactions to pornography also shows that the self-aware group reflected greater compliance to moral standard than the non-self-aware group. In this study, undergraduate female students took a test of sex guilt at the beginning of the semester. The test results reflect the belief that obscene literature helps people become sexual perverts. Later in the semester they were asked to read pornographic literature and rate their enjoyment level. The result revealed that there was no correlation between their earlier belief about obscene literature and sexual perversion and their enjoyment of pornographic literature. However, there was a definite correlation when they were confronted with mirror images. This study supports the belief that attitude guides behavior only when individuals are relatively high on self-awareness.[65]

The previous sections explained how the experience of negativity results in self-focused attention and that self-focused attention results in an awareness of discrepancy. This awareness of the sense that they are not where they ought to be drives depressed individuals to try to affirm themselves through self-regulation. What happens when depressed individuals are engaged in the self-regulatory process? The next chapter will argue that even when depressed individuals lack the ability to attain the desired goals, they are not able to stop this process of self-regulation.

Chapter 5

Self-Regulatory Perseveration
and the Downward Spiral

Why should I go on? I see no light, no end, no way out. No one
beckons me. All that exist are cold, damp walls closing in on
me. Ahead is a useless journey, exhausted step followed by exhausted step, leading deeper into the unknown.

Howard Stone[1]

DEFINING SELF-REGULATORY PERSEVERATION

Self-regulatory perseveration refers to the attempt of the self to
close the gap and attain the goal even though the goal seems unattainable. According to this theory, it is the perseveration of the self in the
regulatory process (reducing the discrepancy) that results in depression. Depression occurs when a person becomes stuck in a self-regulatory cycle in which successful discrepancy reduction is impossible.
When a person is unable to exit, it produces profound psychological
consequences that set in motion a downward spiral of processes that
lead ultimately to depression.[2] This is evident because depressed individuals have a very high level of self-focused attention and tend to
focus on themselves after they fail more than when they succeed.[3] It
is the combination between the high level of self-focused attention and
self-focusing style that makes it difficult for them to disengage from a
"no-longer-attainable life goal" or "the lost object."

Self-regulatory perseveration, explain Pyszczynski and Greenberg,
is a state whereby an individual is obsessed with the lost goal, its
significance to oneself, and ways to regain it.[4] In the language of *wu
wei*, one keeps trying and in the process of trying gets caught in a fu-

tile cycle. Why do depressed people keep on trying even though the goal is unattainable?

TERROR MANAGEMENT THEORY: THE MOTIVE FOR PERSEVERATION

This theory suggests that the need to persist in regulating oneself exists because this unattainable goal provides a central source of self-esteem. Pyszczynski and Greenberg use the terror management theory to support their belief in the centrality of self-esteem as a way of achieving meaning in life. This meaning is defined in relation to depressed individuals' goals that seem unattainable.

Terror management theory asks: What is the motive that drives individuals to be engaged in the self-regulatory process? What do people really want from life that makes them keep pursuing? According to this theory, self-esteem is that motivation. In an experiment conducted with forty-nine introductory psychology students using self-esteem questionnaires, two open-ended questions concerned their thoughts and feelings about death, and essays reflecting foreigners' views of the United States and Americans' reactions to these views showed "that increasing self-esteem decreased the worldview defense."[5]

There are many theories that suggest the connection between self-esteem and depression.[6] But why is self-esteem so important that it can potentially lead to depression? Reflecting on writings of cultural anthropologist Ernest Becker, Pyszczynski and Greenberg suggest:

> According to Becker, the same adaptive human abilities that made it possible for our species to accomplish all that we have accomplished are also the source of some very basic problems that find expression at both individual and cultural levels. Specifically, the abilities to think about cause and effect, to project ourselves into the future and imagine things that have yet to happen, and to take ourselves as the object of our own thought free us from reflexive responsiveness to current environmental stimuli and are part of what makes humans distinct from other species. These advanced intellectual abilities greatly increase the complexity of the behavior of which humans are capable.[7]

This uniquely human ability is also the source of uniquely human problems. The ability for self-awareness makes us aware of our mortality, of death. Human beings become aware that this being, in Heidegger's term, is also "being toward death." As a response to this awareness and because of the instinct for self-preservation, we seek to minimize the terror caused by this awareness of our vulnerability. In responding to this vulnerability, we find self-esteem to be the "chief cultural mechanism" that helps us manage the anxiety about our vulnerability and mortality.[8]

The basis of self-esteem consists of two components. People must have faith in a cultural worldview and accept the values and standards associated with that conception (this is the meaning component of self-esteem). Second, they must also believe that it is possible to meet these cultural standards of value (this is the value component of self-esteem). In so doing, they see themselves as valuable actors in a meaningful universe.[9]

To test this hypothesis, three studies were conducted by Jeff Greenberg, Tom Pyszczynski, Sheldon Solomon, Abram Rosenblatt, Mitchell Veeder, Shari Kirkland, and Deborah Lyon. These studies were designed for the purpose of demonstrating that people cope with the terror evoked by the awareness of the possibility of non-being through self-esteem rooted in one's cultural worldview. The first study shows that Christian subjects, when being manipulated to the awareness of mortality, evaluate fellow Christians more positively and evaluate Jews more negatively. In the second study, when faced with the issue of mortality, people tended to like others who shared a similar worldview than those who differed from them. In the third study, the emphasis on mortality encourages positive evaluation for those who praise one's culture and negative evaluation for those who criticize one's culture. These studies support the hypothesis of terror management theory that self-esteem is the motive that keeps one pursuing the goal which is defined by one's cultural worldview.[10]

In order to deal with one's mortality and vulnerability, self-esteem is sought after because one can face existential terror if one recognizes that there is meaning in being "me" even in the face of death. This meaning emerges when one meets the cultural standards that offer value for oneself. Pyszczynski and Greenberg state the connection of self-evaluation, terror management, and meeting cultural standards:

> If self-awareness sets the stage for existential terror, and if self-esteem provides a buffer against this terror, and if the self-regulatory cycle is a mechanism for maintaining a positive self-concept, then it follows that self-awareness would activate the self-regulatory cycle. Only by engaging a self-regulatory cycle can one become certain that one is, indeed, valuable.[11]

Depressed individuals persist in trying to reduce the discrepancy, because their self-worth depends on their ability to close this gap. The question is, what happens to depressed individuals when they keep on trying and yet experience inability to reduce the discrepancy? The next section argues that this process leads to a downward spiral whereby depressed individuals are trapped in its cycle.

THE DOWNWARD SPIRAL

The attempt to close the gap through self-regulation of depressed individuals often lands them in a cycle of self-perseveration and self-criticism. This is because, while in the process of self-regulation, depressed individuals look at their efforts through the lens of negative self-schema. This is where the negation takes place. This section attempts to show the connection between the persistence of the self in the attempt to reduce discrepancy, even though the goal is unattainable, and the downward spiral of this "trying." According to Pyszczynski and Greenberg, this depressive self-focusing style serves to maintain and exacerbate symptoms of depression. By focusing persistently on the self when negative outcomes occur, the negative psychological impact on the self will be maximized.[12]

Pyszczynski and Greenberg suggest that the negative self-schema is a contributing factor to the downward spiral effect. This depressive self-schema functions to filter internal and external information.[13] It affects the way one receives information and responds or reacts to this information. The coexistence of self-perseveration and the presence of depressive self-schema are important factors that contribute to the downward spiral effects among depressed individuals. This negative self-schema includes self-blame, self-evaluation, negative memory bias, and self-focus after failure.

Self-Blame

The relationship between self-blame and depression is widely recognized. It is viewed as one of the symptoms of depression. It is a phenomenon of depressive illness.[14] Renee-Louise Franche's dissertation attempted measurement of self-criticism and dependency by studying twenty depressed individuals who regained normal functioning and twenty nondepressed individuals. The study showed that remitted and currently depressed individuals exhibited higher levels of self-criticism and interpersonal dependency.[15] Speaking of self-blame, Beck writes, "[T]he depressive's perseverating self-blame and self-criticism appear to be related to his egocentric notions of causality and his penchant for criticizing himself for his alleged deficiencies."[16]

Self-Evaluation

The process of self-evaluation as a result of self-focus is also common among depressed individuals. A number of studies have found that depressed individuals focus on their emotion as a coping method.[17] Studies have also investigated the theory that self-awareness "instigates an evaluative process by which one's standing on a given dimension is compared with whatever standard for that dimension is currently salient."[18] Scheier and Carver's research found that a high level of public self-consciousness is closely related to the tendency to engage in social comparison in the process of self-evaluation. Therefore, they conclude that self-focused attention increases the search for standards necessary for one to evaluate oneself.[19] Consequently, if negative effects often result in greater self-focused attention, then self-evaluation is a natural concomitant to this process. Pyszczynski and Greenberg suggest that a high self-evaluative state resulting from the perseveration of self-regulatory process will undermine self-esteem.[20]

Negative Memory Bias

Increased interest in the study of negative recall among depressed individuals is often based on the belief that this negative memory bias contributes to the development and maintenance of depression and hence contains an important therapeutic implication. Psychologist Paul H. Blaney's review of the empirical literature on the relationship between depression and recall concludes that depressed individuals recall more negative information than nondepressed individuals.[21] A study of the recall of past events based on twelve depressed psychiatric patients by David M. Clark and John D. Teasdale also shows this negative memory bias while experiencing depressed mood.[22] These findings are taken by researchers as evidence of the operation of depressive self-schema.[23]

In their study of the negative memory bias of depressed individuals, Tom Pyszczynski, James Hamilton, Fred H. Herring, and Jeff Greenberg selected forty-seven women and twenty-four men who met the criteria for depression.[24] Subjects were told that the study was concerned with personality assessment and the method used was story writing. First, the subjects were given a booklet that included the BDI, the story-writing task, and a life-events recall questionnaire. The story-writing task was used mainly to manipulate the subjects' attentional focus. The subjects were then asked to list ten events that happened to them in the last two weeks. The result showed that depressed individuals generally recalled more negative than positive events while nondepressed individuals recalled more positive than negative events. It is important to note that the results of this experiment took place after the manipulation of subjects' attentional focus through the story-writing task. It filters out the possibility of differential external circumstances, since this manipulation aimed at intensifying self-awareness, which is in line with the hypothesis that negative memory bias occurs when individuals are self-focused. In other words, self-focused attention of depressed individuals results in negative retrieval of information.

In the second experiment, the same procedure was replicated with two alterations. First the subjects were randomly assigned to recall ten events that had occurred to them or others within the past two weeks. Second, subjects were asked to go back over their responses and rate them as positive, negative, or neutral in affective tone. Results showed that, under the condition of self-focus, depressed subjects' recall of events that happened to themselves were less positive in comparison to nondepressed individuals. Subjects' recall of events happening to others, under self-focused conditions, showed no differences between depressed and nondepressed subjects. However, under the external-focused condition, depressed subjects' recall of events happening to others were less positive.[25]

Self-Focus After Failure

There is increasing interest in studies of depression in the self-focusing style of depressed individuals. Depressed individuals tend to self-focus more after failure than after success. Commenting on this observation, Pyszczynski and Greenberg write, "[P]aradoxically, depressed individuals seem to be constantly oppressed by such perceived deficiencies in themselves, and yet they tend toward more rather than less self-focus than do nondepressed individuals."[26]

In their study of the self-focusing style of depressed individuals,[27] Pyszczynski and Greenberg's chosen subjects for the study were selected based on their BDI scores. Individuals with scores of eight or less were classified as nondepressed, individuals with scores of ten or more were classified as depressed. Thirty-six female and twenty male students were selected within two weeks of the initial screening. Subjects were assigned to fill out a questionnaire and were informed that the study aimed at measuring verbal intellectual abilities. Researchers manipulated the performance outcome by giving half a set of easily solvable anagrams and the other half a set of difficult anagrams. After the completion, the experimenters scored the tests and returned them to the subjects with comments on the performance.

Subjects then were taken to a second room to work on the puzzles. A sign "Mirror Image Study" was placed on the door as they entered the room. The room contained two tables and on each table was a set of puzzles. In front of one of the tables was a large mirror facing the chair. Subjects were asked to work on the puzzle on one table without a mirror and then move to the other table with a mirror. At the completion, the subjects were escorted back to complete a questionnaire that dealt with their ratings of preference for the puzzles, the performance on the anagram, and other questions pertaining to their reactions to the anagram test. Findings show that "depressed subjects liked the mirror-associated puzzle after failure more than did nondepressed subjects and were less likely than nondepressed subjects to choose the mirror associated puzzle after success."[28] Nondepressed subjects, on the other hand, liked the mirror-associated puzzle more after success than failure. A number of other studies have also shown that depressed individuals do not exhibit the self-serving attributional bias that non-depressed individuals usually do.[29] These findings provide us with a clearer understanding of how the tendency toward self-focused attention after failures increases the negating process of the negativity of depression.

When people go through depression, they do not only experience hopelessness, lack of meaning, and negative self-perception. Every attempt they make toward correcting and affirming themselves is negated by self-blame, negative recall, self-focus on failure, and negative attributions. Therefore, in the act of trying, they end up being further removed. It is similar to this salesman's observation:

> When I begin to have some depression [I begin to have] dark thoughts, something bad is going to happen. . . . It's kind of like a black thought process that just begins to kind of take over, and then the anxiety, light-headed, don't feel like eating. These are all symptoms. . . . But when those initial thoughts start to come in regularly, they basically take over. Then it's like life is worthless, and why even bother to get out of bed.[30]

ANALYSIS

In her study of self-structure among depressed individuals, Paula Ray Pietromonaco found that the self-structure of people with depression tends to be less conceptually complex and is organized more around affect and less in terms of other aspects of the self.[31] If it is true that depressed individuals experience negative affect, this self-structure, which is organized around negative affect while disregarding other aspects of the self, will result in the intensification of the experience of negativity and negative self-perception. How will this intensified negativity be experienced? I believe this is an important factor that contributes to the problem of negation and cycles of depression.

Putting this information together, we can see how the negating power of negativity traps one in a depressive cycle. Negative self-perception, one of the symptoms of depression, activates depressive self-schema. Depressive self-schema intensifies one's negative affect, which, in turn, draws attention onto the self. Increased self-awareness leads to self-evaluation and motivates one to try to reduce the discrepancy. This is where negation takes place, and the cycle is perpetuated. Every "trying" is accompanied by the depressive self-schema. Every time one tries to close the gap, one focuses on one's failure, blames oneself, remembers mostly the negatives, and attributes positive outcomes to external factors and negative outcomes to the self. This attempt increases the focus on oneself. This increased focus and the inability to close the gap intensifies negative affects. "The intensified negative affect, self-blame, self-evaluation, and disruption of successful, competent behavior in other domains pushes the recently destabilized self-concept toward negativity."[32] Intensified negative affect, in turn, leads to greater awareness of discrepancy. Awareness of the discrepancy leads to trying and the cycle continues. One recognizes that the cycle is in a downward spiral. This is so because the depressive self-schema negates every attempt to close the gap. The more one tries, the worse one feels toward oneself. The depressive self-schema emerging from this process of trying (self-regulatory perseveration) serves to maintain and exacerbate the depressive symptoms or, as a depressed individual once said, there is a "downward slide and there is no way I can turn it around."[33]

Can the negating power of negativity be dealt with in such a way that depressed individuals will not be trapped in its cycle? We often think that if we were to try harder, we could overcome the experience of negativity. Lao Tzu has a different perspective. He advises:

> When the will to power is in charge, the higher the ideals, the lower the results. Try to make people happy, and you lay the groundwork for misery. Try to make people moral, and you lay the groundwork for vice.[34]

In the next chapter I argue that the principle of *wu wei* can help depressed individuals cope with negativity in a way that can slowly reduce the power of negation inherent in depression.

Chapter 6

Wu Wei

The movement of the Way is a return;
In weakness lies its major usefulness.
From What-is all the world of things was born
But What-is sprang in turn from What-is-not.

Lao Tzu[1]

Chao-Chou asked, "What is the Tao?"
The master [Nan-ch'uan] replied, "Your ordinary conscious-
ness is the Tao."
"How can one return into accord with it?"
"By intending to accord you immediately deviate."
"But without intention, how can one know the Tao?"
"The Tao," said the master, "belongs neither to knowing nor to
not knowing. Knowing is false understanding; not knowing is
blind ignorance. If you really understand the Tao beyond doubt,
it's like the empty sky. Why drag in right and wrong?"

Chuang Tzu[2]

The principle of *wu wei* is paradoxical. It asks us to move forward
by stepping backward. It finds fulfillment in emptiness. This principle seems contradictory to logic. The strange thing is that things seem
to work even when they may sound contradictory. People often seem
to be operating by a kind of logic and reasoning that transcends our
rationality or, in Stanley Cavell's words, "[T]here is something in the
self that logically cannot be brought to knowledge."[3]

I am beginning to realize, as I observe events in life, that what one
needs is to move toward balance and learn to maintain tension. To ap-

ply only logic and seek only to eliminate tension is to uproot the self from its nature. Life is not a logical system. Logic is only one part of life. We cannot define life through rationality, being through logic. Life is to be observed, and through the process of observation, we may come to a better understanding of nature. Through observation, Chinese sages arrived at the understanding that nature is paradoxical. To try to be selfless is to be filled with self. To attempt humility is to attempt an impossibility. To seek love is to push love away. To claim to know God is to know nothing. To want is not to get and to get comes from not wanting. Try to be yourself, and you end up being others. Not trying to be yourself is to find your very own self. Try to be a saint, and you become conscious of your sins. Try to be a sinner, and you realize the saint within. Life is a paradox and perhaps, in our theological construction and for pastoral care, there is much we can learn from Lao Tzu and Chuang Tzu.

> The student learns by daily increment.
> The Way is gained by daily loss,
> Loss upon loss until
> At last comes rest.
>
> By letting go, it all gets done;
> the world is won by those who let it go!
> But when you try and try,
> the world is then beyond the winning.[4]

LAO TZU AND CHUANG TZU

There are many stories surrounding the life of Lao Tzu,[5] especially his authorship of the *Tao Te Ching.* According to the *Records of the Historian,* he was a native of Ch'u (which is now Honan Province). His family name was Li and he served as a custodian of imperial archives. Lao Tzu is also known as Old Tan (Old Boy). It is believed that he was born with white hair. At the age of 160 he became disgusted with moral decay of the Chou dynasty and decided to retire in a better environment. Leaving the kingdom through the Han-Ku Pass, the passkeeper Yin Hsi requested that he compose a book. Lao Tzu wrote more than 5,000 words on the Way *(Tao)* and its Virtue *(Te).*[6] Lao Tzu's Taoism is conceptualized as the Natural Way or the Way of Nature. As a way of life, it denotes simplicity, spontaneity, tranquility, weakness, and non-action *(wu wei).*[7] Herrlee Creel calls Lao Tzu's Taoism "purposive," in that it "is concerned with how one should respond to the world."

Not much is known about the background of Chuang Tzu. According to Ssu-ma Ch'ien's account, his personal name was Chou (Chuang Chou). He came from the district of Meng (which is now Honan). Mencius and he were contemporaries but did not know each other due to geographical separation. Ssu-ma Ch'ien dated Chuang Tzu in the reigns of King Hui of Liang or Wei (370-319 B.C.) and King Hsuan of Ch'i (319-301 B.C.).[8] Chuang Tzu's Taoism is transcendental in nature. While Lao Tzu dealt with the Way within this world, Chuang Tzu moved beyond the realm of the mundane and embraced the transcendence. His Taoism is spontaneous, intuitive, private, and unconventional.

TAOIST PHILOSOPHY

Definition

The Chinese character *Tao* is composed of a head which represents a knowledgeable person and another part which depicts the process of walking. *Tao* is referred to as a road, a path, the way by which people walk, the way of nature that is the ultimate reality. To Chinese mystics, *Tao* means the original undifferentiated Reality.[9] To Lao Tzu, *Tao* is just a name for whatever happens. "The Tao principle is what happens of itself *[tzu-jan].*"[10]

Description

According to Lao Tzu, *Tao* contains all opposites. It contains all opposites because *Tao* is unfathomable, invisible, and inaudible. *Tao* is the one, past and present, form and formless, being and non-being. In describing *Tao* as embracing all opposites, Chung-yuan Chang paraphrases Chuang Tzu's method of comparison by stating, "We all know, as a matter of fact, that size is relative and subject to change.

One stick may be shorter than another and yet longer than a third. Consequently, the stick embraces the apparently opposed qualities of longness and shortness."[11] The attempt to discriminate between short and long, high and low, good and bad, Chuang Tzu calls "three in the morning" and explains its meaning by telling a story about a monkey trainer who handed out food to the monkeys saying, "You get four in the morning and three at night." The monkeys were furious. "Very well then," the trainer responded, "you get three in the morning and four at night." At this, the monkeys were delighted. There was no change in the reality behind the words, but the monkeys responded differently. "Let them be, if they want to," responded Chuang Tzu. But we need to harmonize with right and wrong and allow Heaven to equalize things.[12]

Tao contains all opposites. But *Tao* does not contain only all the opposites. It contains all things. There is nothing excluded from *Tao* as Chuang Tzu has pointed out, "There is nothing that is not the 'that' and there is nothing that is not the 'this.' . . . Therefore I say that the 'that' is produced by the 'this' and the 'this' is also caused by the 'that.'"[13] This is how Chuang Tzu describes *Tao:*

> Tung-kwo Tze asked Kwang-tze, saying,
> "Where is what you call the Tao to be found?"
> Kwang-tze replied, "Everywhere."
> The other said, "Specify an instance of it. That will be more satisfactory."
> "It is here in this ant."
> "Give a lower instance."
> "It is in this panic grass."
> "Give me a still lower instance."
> "It is in this earthenware tile."
> "Surely that is the lowest instance?"
> "It is in that excrement."
> To this Tung-kwo Tze gave no reply.[14]

Tao speaks of wholeness. Lao Tzu illustrates this concept.

> We join spokes together in a wheel,
> but it is the center hole
> that makes the wagon move.

> We shape clay into a pot,
> but it is the emptiness inside
> that holds whatever we want.[15]

From this emptiness comes the function of the wheel. The whole is made possible because of the principle of *Tao*. The whole is made possible because of emptiness. How is this possible? The low empty space makes possible the flow of water. From emptiness comes movement. Lao Tzu said, "All streams flow to the sea because it is lower than they are."[16] This movement of nature is not something we can predict, organize, or categorize. This movement has a life of its own. It is expressed in the concept of *tzu-jan* (things happen by themselves). It is organic. Nature is organic. It has its own definite movement that cannot be captured by the law of geometry. The wave has a pattern, but we cannot capture it. It moves when it wants to move and where it wants to move. It cannot be told what to do. It cannot be labeled as "good" or "bad." It just moves along with the flow of nature. It is "freedom gained in yielding to constant change."[17] This *Tao* is the inner principle that makes all things possible. It is in all things and yet transcends every thing.[18]

THE CONCEPT OF WU WEI

If *Tao* is the Way and this Way is the way of nature, how can we achieve this *Tao*? How can we become a part of this *Tao*? The way of the sage, suggests Lao Tzu, is through *wu wei* (non-action or non-trying).[19] Therefore *wu wei* is the way to the Way. As already implied in the term *wu wei* (non-action, non-doing, or non-trying), we cannot try become a part of the Tao. To try to become a part of the *Tao* is to pursue an illusion. We cannot become, because we are already a part of. To try to become is to depart further. To not try through non-doing is an invitation to return to who we are, to ourselves, to the *Tao*. *Wu wei* takes us to the Way.

Wu is literally translated, "not" or "no." *Wei* means "do." Hence *wu wei* may be translated as "not doing."[20] Sometimes it is used as "*wei wu wei*," which can be translated "doing without doing or trying without trying." The concept of *wu wei* is expressed through the writings of both Lao Tzu and Chuang Tzu. However, Chuang Tzu provides a clearer expression of this concept. This is also the reason this concept is more difficult to grasp. Chuang Tzu's writing is filled with mystery, humor, and irony. We may find the concept of *wu wei* puzzling, but it is hauntingly crucial.

In the following section, I will first try to clarify a common misunderstanding and then proceed to identify how we have departed from the Way in order to understand how we can return to the Way through *wu wei*.

A Common Misunderstanding

Speaking of *wu wei*, Daisetz Teitaro Suzuki warns, "The doctrine of *wu wei* is one stumbling block that puzzles Western minds in their first study of Oriental thought."[21] Suzuki points out the dualistic nature of thinking that dominates the Western world as a stumbling block to the understanding of nonaction in Taoism. Another common misunderstanding is to view *wu wei* as passivity. *Wu wei* is not about doing nothing. It is about non-doing. Non-doing is to do without an effort. It is effortless because it is spontaneous action. This spontaneous act of *wu wei* is best illustrated in the story of cook Ting as told by Chuang Tzu.

> A cook was cutting up an ox for Lord Wenhui. . . . Each slice of the cleaver was right in tune, zip zap! He danced in rhythm to "The Mulberry Grove," moved in concert with the strains of "The Managing Chief." "Ah, wonderful!" said Lord Wenhui, "that skill can attain such heights!"

What is the secret of cook Ting? This is his explanation to Lord Wenhui:

> A good cook changes his cleaver once a year because he chops. An ordinary cook changes his cleaver once a month because he hacks. Now I've been using my cleaver for nineteen years and have cut up thousands of oxen with it, but the blade is still as fresh as though it had just come from the grindstone. Between the joints there are spaces, but the edge of the blade has no thick-

ness. Since I am inserting something without any thickness into an empty space, there will certainly be lots of room for the blade to play around in. That's why the blade is still as fresh as though it had just come from the grindstone.[22]

From this story we can at least do away with the common misconception that *wu wei* is passivity. *Wu wei* "makes all doing possible."[23] *Wu wei* authenticates our acts.

Departing from the Way

The meaning of *wu wei* will become clearer when we understand how we have departed from the Way, the *Tao*. If nonbeing is the principle behind movements in the phenomenal world, departing from the Way takes place when we place Being as the supreme reality. There is a definite consequence in making Being the reality. While nonbeing accommodates being and nothingness, Being, when it becomes the reality, resists nothingness. If Being is real, than nonbeing is nonreal. When Being becomes the reality, it has to be something and not nothing. To be something requires categories by which one can compare oneself.

We see this process in Heidegger's *Being and Time*. Heidegger started his analysis by using the term *dasein*, which is translated as "human being." The concept of Being is a good starting point because human beings are in a constant quest for Being. Human beings find themselves as already being there in the world.[24] Heidegger calls this the facticity of human beings. In finding themselves as already being-there-in-the-world they also recognize the contingency of being. In discovering itself as being in the world, being is also aware of its being toward death, the temporality of being. This concept of temporality implies orientation toward the future. In finding itself to be in the world with death as its inescapable end, being becomes aware of its contingent nature. It realizes that it has nothing for its basis. This awareness stirs from within the feeling of anxiety and dread *(angst)*.[25] Through anxiety and dread that arise from the awareness of the contingent nature of being, guilt is experienced. This is the guilt of *dasein*, which "succumbs to its inauthenticity in the world."[26] It is the guilt that produces the feeling of insecurity within humanity. This feeling of guilt speaks of having fallen away from authentic life. One is not what one ought to be. Guilt "is the sense of the discrepancy between the given past and the whole I ought to, but never can, create of it."[27] Through guilt, being realizes the inauthenticity of itself. At the very same time, the feeling of guilt always points to something transcendental. Thus, through guilt, human beings become aware of their disunity with Being. This falling away from the origin, from Being, creates within human beings a sense of insecurity. In the search for security, "care" is cultivated. It is through "care" that one strives toward oneness with Being. But to be at-oneness with Being one needs to know Being. The path toward the discovery of Being is directed within.

Conscience is a place where humanity seeks the reconciliation of guilt. Through conscience, one constructs one's knowledge of God, and through this conscience, one constructs the criteria of good and evil. Through conscience, one places before oneself the law of good and evil. One needs to know what is good and what is evil, so that one can do the good and avoid the evil. One needs to do that which is good and avoid that which is evil, in order to get rid of one's guilt and pacify one's conscience. The call of conscience is also the call to destiny, for "destiny is a pattern achieved only by the rare individual who in dread and silence has come face to face with his own nothingness and has shaped his life in the light, or the darkness, of that encounter."[28] In Heidegger's *Being and Time,* we learn that in attempting to be something and not nothing, the self, through conscience, sets standards as a way of authenticating oneself.[29]

To be something is not to be nothing. To be something requires that we set up criteria through which we can affirm that we are something and not nothing. To set up criteria in order to affirm being is the first step in parting from the *Tao* because to do so is to move from unity to polarity. In so doing we move from the basic understanding of the "this" is the "that" to the "this" is the "this" and the "that" is the "that."[30] From criteria comes separation. It turns *yin* and *yang* into two antagonistic forces. It moves from spontaneity to self-consciousness. It reminds us of Jung's understanding of the emergence of consciousness. In my estimation, Jung is suggesting that ego emerges from consciousness. Consciousness leads to logic that is employed to create distinction. In logic, opposites cannot be harmonized and hence, consciousness leads one to the quest for the divine that does not exist. This process reflects the self that has been uprooted from nature itself. In *The Undiscovered Self,* Jung writes:

> Nothing estranges man more from the ground plan of his instincts than his learning capacity. . . . It is also the source of numerous psychic disturbances and difficulties occasioned by man's progressive alienation from his instinctual foundation, i.e., by his *uprootedness* and identification with his conscious knowledge of himself, by his concern with consciousness at the expense of the unconscious.[31]

Entering the world of being (where being takes primacy over nonbeing) results in discriminating and evaluating because the world of being resists nonbeing. One becomes conscious of right and wrong, good and bad. Through this consciousness, one seeks the right and good in an attempt to affirm being. "As a result," states Livia Kohn, "human beings impose their conceptions and wills on nature, instead of following it along."[32] In imposing our conceptions and wills on nature, spontaneity is lost. In its place come rigid codes of behavior. Logic has now replaced nature. Life is now informed by reasoning and thinking becomes the tool. Now we try to tell the wave how to roll and the wind where to flow. The *Tao* is lost and in its place we find the goddess of reason and experience Jung's warning: "Hence it is quite natural that with the triumph of the Goddess of Reason a general neuroticizing of modern man should set in."[33] And we know we have departed from the Way.

Returning to the Way (Wu Wei)

In believing that *yu* (being) is the Way, we *wei* (do) as an attempt to fight the *wu* (nothing). We *wei* through knowledge and rationality. We *wei* by discriminating between good and bad, right and wrong, being and nothing.[34] Through *wei-ing* we have lost our spontaneity. If we depart from the Way through *wei-ing,* perhaps we can return to the Way by *wu-ing* the *wei.* Lao Tzu writes "The *Tao* never does anything, yet through it all things are done."[35]

As stated earlier, we do, we strive, and we try, because we believe that *yu* is the Way. If *yu* (being) is the Way then *yu* is that toward which we must strive. To strive for *yu* is to avoid the *wu.* There are two difficulties we face when we pursue this. First, to avoid the *wu* is to ignore nature itself. Nature is both *wu* and *yu*. It is being and nonbeing. To go against nature is to become unnatural. We see this in our daily lives. We try to deny death through attempting to prolong life. We seek beauty and despise ugliness. We love pleasure and hate pain. We crave success and shun failure. We want to be something and not nothing. We crave the *yu* and avoid the *wu*. Kuang-ming Wu describes this process:

> When one is in the flux of things, life is seen as opposed to death, good to evil, success to failure, being to nothing. In this situation, one usually rallies oneself with all one's might on the side of life to fight off death, strives toward good and away from evil, loves success and abhors failure.[36]

When this takes place we keep moving against the progress of nature because nature is both *yu* and *wu*. Nature is *yin* and *yang*. This leads to the second difficulty. There is *yin* in every *yang* and *yang* in every *yin*. These two are in mutual agreement. They complement each other. The pursuit of *yu* is the pursuit of *yin* without the *yang*, which is an impossibility. An extreme pursuit of *yin* lands one in the *yang* and vice versa. The pursuit of being only creates greater awareness of nothingness. This awareness leads to greater anxiety. Anxiety results in more *wei-ing*. *Wei-ing* intensifies our awareness of the *wu*-ness in us and the cycle goes on.

How can we move out of this cycle? Lao Tzu teaches:

> In the pursuit of knowledge,
> Every day something is added.
> In the practice of the Tao,
> every day something is dropped.
> Less and less do you need to force things,
> until finally you arrive at non-action.
> When nothing is done,
> nothing is left undone.
>
> True mastery can be gained
> by letting things go their own way.
> It can't be gained by interfering.[37]

This process becomes clearer when we turn to the writings of Chuang Tzu. In describing Chuang Tzu's understanding of a free individual, Watson writes:

> He remains within society but refrains from acting out of the motives that lead ordinary men to struggle for wealth, fame, success, or safety. He maintains a state that Chuang Tzu refers to as *wu wei*, or inaction, meaning by this term not a forced quietude, but a course of action that is not founded upon any purposeful motives of gain or striving. In such a state, all human actions become as spontaneous and mindless as those of the natural world. Man becomes one with Nature, or Heaven, as Chuang Tzu calls it, and merges himself with Tao, or the Way, the underlying unity that embraces man, Nature, and all that is in the universe.[38]

Wu wei, therefore, is not trying to be something or trying to avoid being nothing. When we stop trying to be something, we stop making standards whereby we can judge ourselves. When we stop discriminating, we just stop and stay where we are. We stay with nature. We stay with the *Tao*. Masao Abe, a Japanese philosopher, comments, "Tao is never away from us even for a moment. If it is, it is not Tao."[39] We are able to stay where we are, because we have come to realize the primacy of nonbeing over being. We realize that life is about being and nothing. In this recognition, we learn that "[W]e must not fight our opposite, because the opposite is essentially part of ourselves. In this respect, the elimination of the opposite is none other than the elimination of ourselves."[40] As such, we realize that "nothing" is as essential as being. We realize that "nothing" is what makes possible movement in life and nature. Realizing that "nothing" is as essential as being, we see that we do not have to be something. We just need to be who we are. We need to return to our natural selves. We can return, suggests Chuang Tzu, through the process of mind-fasting.

> Mind-fasting is a discipline of mind-divesting, a divesting of those varied self-defeating passions for any single pole of the ontological contrasts in life. One vainly craves talents, sensory pleasures, emotions, knowledge, and morals, and one vainly strives to avoid their lack or their opposites. And yet one's lust traps one in much ado about nothing; the more one tries for

these things, the farther away they are from one, and in the end one destroys oneself in futility.[41]

When we fast our minds, we learn to become one with nature. In becoming one with nature, we flow along with the natural flow of nature. In this flow, one has to do what one cannot help but do because when one follows the flow, one becomes fully spontaneous. The dog barks. The cat meows. The heaven is high. The valley is low.[42] In doing what one cannot help but do, there is no definite form and pattern. There is no exact mode of behavior. There is no rigid standard of character. There is no telling what this being ought to be.[43] In contrasting Aristotle's concept of being with that of Chuang Tzu's, Chenyang Li writes:

> For Chuang Tzu, things have their ways of being. A thing can be a "this" and a "that." While being a "this" is a way for it to be, being a 'that' is another way of its being. Nevertheless, they are different ways for the same object to be. Thus, from his point of view, not only is the world a world of diversity, but also the being of an object is a diversity. One thing we can learn from Chuang Tzu is to open our mind to the diversity of the being of objects, and allow an object to have both "this" and "that," and possibly any number of ways, as its real being.[44]

What can we say about a person who practices *wu wei?* The individuals who have practiced *wu wei* are comfortable with who they are. They are able to engage with others but not be affected by their opinions of them. They do not have the urge to strive to be successful or to avoid failure. They are comfortable with pleasure as with pain, with darkness as with light, with joy as with sorrow. They take life as it comes, doing what they can do in the moment. They can move along adapting with the movement of life.

Individuals who practice *wu wei* also understand that life works in a paradoxical manner. One cannot try to be happy. Happiness happens to the self. One cannot try to be selfless because in an attempt to be selfless one becomes more conscious of oneself. One learns to forget the motive for success and happiness and just do what comes along in life. One even learns that one cannot try not to try.[45]

Chapter 7

Wu Wei, Trying, and Non-Trying

I take inaction to be true happiness,
but ordinary people think it is a bitter thing.

Chuang Tzu

This chapter provides a more in-depth analysis of the relationship between *wu wei* and "trying" in the writings of Chuang Tzu as articulated by Kuang-ming Wu. Wu translates *wu wei* to mean "trying that is no trying."[1] Chuang Tzu believes that authentic human life does not consist of "tries." Therefore, the aim of human life is the "self-emancipation from a 'trying' conflict of two selves through the process of reduction."[2] The two selves here refer to the empirical self and the reflexive self.[3] The term "reduction" means a return to the original self. To return involves removing obstacles along the way.

THE TWO SELVES

The two selves here refer to the empirical self and the reflexive self. By empirical self, Wu refers to the physical self, our body. The reflexive self refers to the self that passes judgment, the self that thinks and reflects. Autonomy is destroyed when the empirical self takes control of the reflexive self (as in brainwashing techniques). When the reflexive self takes control of the empirical self, the self is destroyed because this self becomes a slave to logic. Life is much more than just logic. Chuang Tzu is concerned with the empirical self coming under the control of reflexive self because, to him, this is the problem of modern civilization.[4] What is Chuang Tzu's concern regarding the control of the reflexive self over the empirical self? What happens when consciousness, through the cognitive instrument, decides to take over and dictate one's life? Wu's answer is contained in his understanding of the prereductive self.

THE PREREDUCTIVE SELF

The prereductive self is the self that comes under the control of thoughts and judgment. The context of the reflexive self is one's social setting. Within this context, one finds standards of excellence and is obligated to adhere to these standards. Therefore, being mindful of standards, one judges webbed human toes and a sixth finger on human hands to be contrary to "what ought to be." Here the reflexive self judges webbed toes and the sixth finger as abnormal. The natural becomes deformed, under the scrutiny of the cognitive process for, according to the standards set by the society, webbed toes and the sixth fingers are out of the norm. They are abnormal.[5] "But," Chuang Tzu inquires, "are they really?" In telling the story of webbed toes, Chuang Tzu writes:

> That which is ultimately correct does not lose the characteristics of its nature and destiny. Therefore, joining is accomplished without a web, branching is accomplished without extraneousness, lengthening is accomplished without a surplus, shortening is accomplished without inadequacy. Thus, although a duck's legs are short, if we extend them it will come to grief; although a crane's legs are long, if we cut them short, it will be tragic. Therefore, if what by nature is long is not cut short, and if what by nature is short is not extended, there will be no grief to dispense with.[6]

For this reason, webbed toes and extra fingers are superfluous to one's integrity according to Chuang Tzu.[7] Similar problems occur when a moral person tries to correct moral depravity. In so doing, that person does more harm to the natural way of life.[8] This point illustrates Chuang Tzu and Lao Tzu's belief that conflict is created when we try to grasp nature conceptually. Nature cannot be conceived conceptually. Nature can be learned but not taught. Nature is bigger than what the mind can conceive, what words can describe. Nature "is."

History is filled with stories of people seeking to grasp and define nature. In seeking to define nature, we limit "nature" to that which we can conceive, that which can be categorized in human terms. In seeking to grasp "nature," we limit "nature" to thought forms derived from our vocabulary. Having arrived at what "nature" is, we stipulate the "ought" and dictate how beings should behave. We tell "us" what we ought to be, what we ought to feel. We tell ourselves that if we were other than what we have conceived ourselves to be, then perhaps we are not in line with "nature." We tell ourselves that if we were to feel other than that which we have defined, perhaps we are not feeling right. We seek to define "nature" and allow this definition to dictate our mode of being. Chuang Tzu warns, "ordinary men discriminate among them (right and wrong) and parade their discriminations before others. So I say, those who discriminate fail to see."[9]

The problem emerges because we like to set standards of what ought to be. "The standard induces antagonism between the clever and the stupid, the righteous and the wicked, and the rich and the poor. . . . Such discrimination prostitutes people into 'trying' and 'laboring' to reach the dangled prize of excellence, which now 'enslaves' them."[10]

In setting standards, we try hard to attain the positive and avoid the negative. In this trying, discriminating becomes essential. This discrimination is based on the human attempt to define what one ought to be. The reflexive cognitive definition is often something we impose on nature itself. As a result we destroy human autonomy. Chuang Tzu teaches:

> He who is contending for a piece of earthenware puts forth all his skill. If the prize be a buckle of brass, he shoots timorously; if it be for an article of gold, he shoots as if he were blind. The skill of the archer is the same in all the cases; but he is under the influence of solicitude, and looks on the external prize as most important. All who attach importance to what is external show stupidity in themselves.[11]

When we are enticed by various forms of "excellence," the total self becomes enmeshed in the precarious and entrapping game of "trying."[12] This is so because this "trying," as a process of self-evaluation, is cognitively defined. In trying to fit nature into our thought process, we only do harm to ourselves. We move further away from the natural.[13] The more we try, the more we feel as if something is not right. This feeling that something is not right is met with greater trying, thinking that perhaps in trying harder we can fix this "something which is not right." The harder we strive the more trapped we are, and we learn that there is no satisfactory solution to the problem. Depressed individuals are familiar with the feeling of being trapped. A female nurse describes her experience.

> A sense of being trapped, or being caged, sort of like an animal, like a tiger pacing in a cage. That's sort of how I feel. I feel like I'm in a cage and I'm trapped, and I can't get out and it's night time and the daylight's never going to come. . . . Sometimes I feel like I'm being smothered in that I can't breathe. I am being suffocated. . . . And it's like falling down a well, like I'm free-falling. That's what it is.[14]

In this entrapment, we seek a way out in order to ease the pain. Wu proposes three ways to cope with this cyclical game of trying that enslaves. First, one can try to try. When we feel or think as though we have not attained what we "ought to be," we try harder. The harder we try, the more conscious we become of the gap between the "is" and the "ought." We become more aware of the fact that we have not reached the goal. In trying to try, one often ends up overexerting oneself and depleting oneself of the fullness of life. Perfection is unreal. The real implies the assimilation of both the good and the evil, success and failure.

Second, one can try not to try. "Seeing that the attempt to try only injures oneself, one can try to stop trying."[15] But to try to stop trying is another form of trying. It is "trying not to try." One still gets caught, because one still remains within the same paradigm that defines the self. Take, for example, a person who believes that to be sociable one needs to be casual; he or she then tries to attain this state of being. In the process of trying, the person becomes more conscious of trying to be casual. Being conscious of the attempt, the person becomes conscious of not being casual enough, because to be casual presupposes spontaneity and which presupposes a lack of self-consciousness. Becoming more aware that this is not working, the person may try to not try to be conscious only to realize that "trying" is a conscious act. Where there is trying, there is consciousness. Where there is consciousness there is no spontaneity. Hence, a person who tries not to try is still caught in the game of trying. This person does not realize that being casual is a state whereby a person does not even need to try to be or to try not to be, but to just "be" without the awareness of what one "ought to be." When one tries not to try, one is still caught within the power of "trying." One is not free from it. It is only a form of negation that presupposes the existence of "trying."

Finally, one can just give up on trying. This implies a sense of despair. It is the acceptance of the condemned self that is unable to attain the desired goal. It is the self remaining caught within the dualistic paradigm of the "this" and the "that." It is giving up on the self, which is not the same as *wu wei* or to achieve by not trying.

These three ways, argues Wu, cannot release us from the cycle and the trap that we find ourselves in because, within this paradigm, one realizes that "no matter which way one turns, one is trapped in the terrible irrelevance of 'trying' to push the boat across the land; both the boat (the self) and the land (nature) are hurt."[16] Here Wu agrees with Edmund Husserl in suggesting that it is the "empiricistic prejudice that prevents one from seeing things as they are. . . . Obsessive conation drives oneself out of touch with oneself and with reality."[17]

THE REDUCTIVE SELF

Chuang Tzu teaches that reduction is a way out of the dilemma of "to try" or "not to try." Getting out of this dilemma means returning to the place prior to any construction of presuppositions or worldview. It is viewing the world without a preconceived notion about the world. To achieve this, the whole cognitive area needs to be "bracketed."

"The 'activity' of leaving the realm of activity is neither a cessation of activity nor an activity alongside other activities. It is instead a reflexive self-activity, a metaeffort that culminates in effortlessness."[18] But there are the three contrasts that keep us within the cycle of "trying." These contrasts are: doing and non-doing, speech and silence, and knowledge and ignorance.

Doing and Non-Doing

What does Chuang Tzu mean by doing and non-doing? Nondoing is the exact opposite of doing. But this is not what Chuang Tzu has in mind. It is not a doing nothing but a non-doing, a *wu wei*. *Wu wei* is the non-doing that leaves nothing undone. Non-doing, therefore, refers to that doing which does not require one to use effort. It is not forcing things to happen. It is doing that seeks to flow along with the flow of nature itself.

Speech and Silence

Regarding speech and silence, we often contrast these two in our daily life. That person speaks. That person keeps silence. In such a contrast, one becomes better than the other. Chuang Tzu is suggesting something very different from our ordinary dichotomy. He is suggesting that in silence we speak and in speech we communicate silence. There is such a profoundness to silence that in our encounter with this silence we experience profound understanding. At the very same time there is the speech that speaks to us of the depth of silence. "When one grows 'sensitive to the thread of silence from which the tissue of speech is woven,' one can remain silent and forever speak, and conversely, whenever one speaks, one can speak silence."[19]

Knowledge and Ignorance

Chuang Tzu admonishes us to move away from the dichotomy of knowledge and ignorance. The dichotomy between craving for knowledge and avoidance of ignorance, too, must be avoided. What we need to seek is that quiet discernment that remains between knowledge and ignorance since it is ignorance that makes understanding meaningful. The relationship between knowledge and ignorance is like the relationship between the feet and the empty space on the ground. It takes empty space for one to be able to move forward. Similarly, it takes ignorance to move one further into greater understanding. Because, as Chuang Tzu says, "understanding that rests in what it does not understand is the finest."[20] Appreciation of ignorance is a prerequisite for the appreciation of truth. "The great tragedy is that 'no one understands enough to rely upon what understanding does not understand and thereby come to understand.' "[21] To accept our ignorance is to be opened. When one is opened one can see things more clearly because one has ceased to impose the cognitive category of "what life ought to be" on being and allow being to speak for itself. To allow being to speak to us is to allow it to reveal itself. "Being" reveals itself when we stop trying to force "being" into a certain mode of being but allow the self to experience that which is and through this "isness" come to an understanding of the self.

> To borrow from Heidegger for our purpose, an artist lets manifest the Is of what-Is in its sheer presence, which is the life of reality standing-out (exist, in answer to "subjective" reduction) of the humdrum ordinary routine. The presence presents itself. . . . The presence is also that creative enriching power of reality, a "con" forming thrust of Reality (the Presence) with reality (self's presence), more a corresponsiveness with reality than a passive correspondence to it. In this sense, the self is, via its being open (cognitively and conatively), an active co-creator and co-revealer of reality. The self is a phenomenon of life, an active phenomenology of truth.[22]

Summary and Conclusions

To heed Chuang Tzu's advice is to move away from the three contrasts that initiate the self into the process of "trying."[23] If there is no "better," then there is no "worse." If it can neither get better nor worse, one need not try. Wu summarizes:

> In short, one must go out of the three realms of contrast — doing and not doing, speech and silence, knowledge and ignorance. This is because the contrasts are indicative of contentious disturbances within the self, of a discord between the reflexive self and the empirical. They are caused by the reflexive self's stubborn effort to gain control over the totality of the self, with its 'good' intention to benefit life and 'help [improve] nature' (of the empirical self). Yet the harder the reflexive self tries, the fiercer does the internal contention grow between knowledge and stupidity, speech and silence, trying and not trying.[24]

Reduction is a return to nature. To return to nature one needs to learn the art of emptying. Emptying is achieved when one can look at the world without any preunderstanding. Once emptied, one can look at and appreciate the world as it is. To illustrate this, Chuang Tzu points out that people try to escape from pain and sorrow, not realizing that both pain and sorrow are a part of life. Similarly, Tillich believes that anxiety is the fundamental quality of human beings. It is the inward expression of outward finitude. Ontological anxiety is beyond the power of psychotherapy to remove, since it is occasioned by the unchangeable structure of human finitude. Therefore, one cannot aim at the removal of ontological anxiety. To try to remove this anxiety is to attempt the restructuring of human finitude.[25]

Who can escape pain and sorrow? When we can look at things just as they are, we will be able to accept and try to live our lives in accordance with what is.

THE POSTREDUCTIVE SELF

Reduction is a method that seeks to engage life by disengaging. In what way does this method disengage us and in what way does it engage us in life? Reduction disengages us from the dichotomy of the empirical and reflexive self. Through reduction, there is no longer the need for the reflexive self to seek control over the empirical self and vice versa. There is no need to control, because the need does not exist. The need to control emerges only as a result of the self's inability to affirm itself as it is. And the need to affirm leads to the desire to self-evaluate, which results in comparing oneself with standards and, hence, to the existence of the three contrasts. But, when one fasts, contrasts no longer exist. The self does not have to strive to be what it thinks it ought to be. It affirms itself in the current present condition. It is good enough. We hear similar theological reflection in the writings of Dietrich Bonhoeffer. In *Ethics,* Bonhoeffer writes, "[T]he first task of Christian ethics is to invalidate this knowledge (knowledge of good and evil)."[26] Only the Creator knows good and evil. To think in terms of good and evil is to seek to ordain the path for ourselves. It is to be a Creator. This is the limit of creatures. We are limited by the fact that we cannot ordain our own path without going against the structure of our beings, our essence.[27] Such a realization puts a stop to the reflexive self's desire to take control over the empirical self.

On the other hand, it is through this disengagement that one becomes fully engaged in life. When one does not have to struggle between trying and not trying, one can stay in the midst of turmoil. When one stops trying to tell life how it should be and where it should go, one can become engaged with every changing circumstance. One can flow along by changing circumstances and, sometimes, by changing with them. This becomes a possibility because one learns to take things as they are, "neither violating them nor being violated by them."[28]

This process of disengaging has a healing psychological and spiritual effect. If emotional trauma and pain are caused by conflict that emerges from "being" resisting to be defined through rational process or placed into a logical system, then finding "Being" by allowing this "being" to speak can potentially bring about the relief of psychological trauma and emotional pain in one's life. When we are trying to "be" what we are not, believing that "who we are not" is "who we really are," then life and our internal psychic process turns against us. By so doing, we block the natural flow of our psyche and our life. We become enemies to ourselves. Blocking of the natural flow is exhibited in various forms. In describing the inhibition of the natural grief process Kaplan, Sadock, and Grebb write:

> Grief that is inhibited or denied expression is potentially pathogenic because the bereaved person avoids dealing with the reality of the loss. . . . Inhibited or denied grief reactions contain the seeds of such unfortunate consequences as experiencing persistent physical symptoms similar to those of the deceased person and unaccountable reactions on the anniversary of the loss or on occasions of significance to the deceased.[29]

The above is one example of the many possible ways we damage our psyche if we resist the natural flow of life. In describing the Taoist sage, Lao Tzu writes, "The Master does nothing, yet he leaves nothing undone."[30] Similarly Chuang Tzu states:

> I have heard of letting the world be, and exercising forbearance; I have not heard of governing the world. Letting be is from the fear that men (when interfered with), will carry their nature beyond its normal condition; exercising forbearance is from the

fear that men (when not so dealt with), will alter the characteristics of their nature. When all men do not carry their nature beyond its normal condition, nor later its characteristics, the good government of the world is secured.[31]

Prior to the process of reduction, the self experienced conflict within itself and with the world. It was the self divided against itself and, for this reason, it was not able to become flexible. It could not move, because it sought to tell life how it should be. This lack of flexibility disallowed a person to be engaged in life and reality. But a person who has been engaged through disengagement is able to participate fully. The world and life activities remain the same for this person and yet, in all its sameness, a radical transformation has occurred.

The transformation takes place on the attitudinal level. In this place, the self tries without trying and achieves without doing because one's action becomes spontaneous. It is effortless because it does what cannot be helped.[32] An individual who does what cannot be helped, according to Chuang Tzu, is a mature person. A mature person is a person who forgets. When we forget our feet, our shoes seem to fit. When we forget our waists, our belt seems to fit. Forgetting the knowledge of right and wrong brings comfort to the soul. Forgetting the need for approval, we feel comfortable within society. When we forget in the *wu wei* sense, the distinction between the "is" and the "ought to be" is forgotten. The forgotten distinction brings harmony to what is. The self returns to itself. Through this forgetfulness one returns to oneself, and play becomes a possibility. One can play because one needs not try, and play becomes a possibility since it is an act of irresistible spontaneity. This is the self that plays as it moves within the natural flow of things. It can play because the "trying" stops and the self emerges, fully engaged.[33] This self speaks of truth in being itself. It is. And it remains true to what it is. "Tao or Truth," writes Abe, a Japanese philosopher, "is not over there, is not something to be realized in the future, but is right here, right now, in our ordinary mind."[34]

EMPTINESS

The principle of *wu wei* encourages us to practice non-doing. To "non-do" is to empty ourselves of cognitive construction as a means toward self-affirmation or as an attempt to cope with the anxiety of nonbeing. Therefore, the practice of emptiness is a very important process in the art of non-doing. "Just be empty, that's all," said Chuang Tzu. "The mind of the ultimate man functions like a mirror. It neither sends off nor welcomes; it responds but does not retain. Therefore, he can triumph over things without injury."[35] This emptying process keeps one from pondering over praise and blame, life and death, knowledge and ignorance, speech and silence. Here one recognizes that one no longer needs to affirm oneself through the process of self-evaluation. When the "isness" of the self is affirmed, evaluation by comparison is not needed. When the self realizes that this self does not have to strive for what it ought to be, the "trying" process ceases. The cycle ends. We hear the echo of Buddha's teaching very clearly in this context. One must aim for *anatta* ("no-self") if one is to exit the cycle of *samsara* (the cycle of birth and rebirth). Only the emptied self can exit the cycle.[36]

In emptying, one becomes full, because emptiness swallows desire for gain and approval. When the self does not need to gain, there is no fear of loss. When the self does not need approval, there is no fear of disapproval. One can now act at will. Spontaneity emerges. This self will do what it cannot help but do, and whatever it does will be in accord with what it ought to do.[37]

Therefore, to exit this cycle of "trying" through the process of self-evaluation one needs to empty oneself of the contrasts and theories that have been created by the cognitive self in an attempt to correct or affirm itself, because "theorizing" is the reflexive self's way of dominating the empirical self. For this reason, one must enter the process of reduction through fasting oneself and emptying all the internal disturbances. This is the way out of the vicious cycle.

However, it is important to have a clear understanding of the concept of emptiness as articulated by Lao Tzu and Chuang Tzu before we can encourage others to enter this process. To be emptied here does not mean to have no self but to return to the natural self as is. There is a tendency to interpret emptiness as a process of emptying our worth, our feelings, our opinions, even our sense of identity in ourselves. But when *wu wei* invites us to emptiness, it invites us to empty any construct we may have regarding how to be good and avoid being bad. If a woman were told that in expressing her opinions she is not being feminine, *wu wei* invites her to empty this construct that associates expression of opinions with a lack of femininity. If she naturally gravitates toward the expression of opinions, then that is who she really is and that is what she should be. To be otherwise is to be inauthentic. When she tries to be feminine as defined by others, she is caught in a conflict. The activity that she engages in is the very activity that disengages her from her self. Hence, the ability to empty herself of this construct determines the quality of her self-engagement or as Abe writes, "emptiness is not a mere emptiness but rather fullness."[38] This concept of emptiness is clarified in the dialogue between Chuang Tzu and Hui Tzu:

> Hui Tzu asked Chuang Tzu if a person can be without feelings. Chuan Tzu said, "Yes."
> "If a person has no feelings, how can you call that person a human being?" asked Hui Tzu.
> "Heaven gave this person a form and so why can't we call this person a human being?" replied Chuang Tzu.
> "But if you called this person a human being, this person can not be without feelings?" protested Hui Tzu.
> "This is not how I define feelings," said Chuang Tzu. "Not having feelings means that this person does not allow likes and dislikes to harm her. She just lets things be they way they are refusing to try to help life move in a certain direction."
> "If she doesn't help life along, how can she keep herself alive?" asked Hui Tzu.
> "Heaven gave this person a form and she does not allow likes and dislikes to harm her. But you deal with your soul as if it is something external to you. You wear out your energy by grumbling and slumping at your desk dozing. Heaven gave you a body and you use this body trying to distinguish between 'hard' and 'white.'" replied Chuang Tzu. [39]

How can we apply this principle of emptiness to the problem of the negativity of depression? How does this fit into the discussion of the self-regulatory perseveration theory and the sustaining ministry of pastoral care for depressed individuals fighting the negativity of depression? Chapter 8 will explore these issues.

Chapter 8

Wu Wei and the Sustaining Ministry of Pastoral Care

> Change takes place, but not according to plan or as the result of intentional intervention. If you attend the soul closely enough, with an educated and steadfast imagination, changes take place without your being aware of them until they are all over and well in place. Care of the soul observes the paradox whereby a muscled, strong-willed pursuit of change can actually stand in the way of substantive transformation.
>
> Thomas Moore[1]

Among Asian religions such as Buddhism, Hinduism, and Taoism, the concept of the vicious cycle is a common theme. Each religion aims at providing believers a way out of this vicious cycle of pain and suffering. Although this vicious cycle is often described within religious belief systems as metaphysical in nature, I believe that it can be translated into psychological and existential terms as well. The pain of depression can also be expressed as the pain of being caught in a cycle of self-evaluation and self-criticism. The principle of *wu wei*, I have argued, can offer relief for individuals caught in this cycle triggered by the negativity of depression.

SUSTAINING MINISTRY

The term pastoral care is derived from the biblical image of shepherding and aims at providing care from the context of religious community to persons in distress. The distress is often experienced in relation to the struggle of the soul. Pastoral care, therefore, is concerned with providing care for the soul in distress. How does one provide care for the soul? Pastoral theologian Seward Hiltner outlines three functions of pastoral care: healing, sustaining, and guiding.[2] As shepherds, the soul must be the center of these functions in that, ultimately, these functions must lead to the question of meaning and reality.[3]

What then is the sustaining ministry of pastoral care? The term sustaining, in the pastoral care context, may be defined as an attempt "to console and strengthen; to stand alongside to lend support and encouragement when the situation cannot be changed, at least not immediately; to carry on a ministry of sustenance as long as circumstances preclude healing."[4] Although the aim of pastoral care is to bring distressed individuals to wholeness, there are times when this may not be possible or, at least, not in the near future. This is the period that calls for the sustaining ministry of pastoral care. "Thus," writes LeRoy Aden, "sustaining is a distinct ministry, important in its own right, though it also presses toward healing when that is possible."[5] The experience of negativity among depressed individuals is not something that can be immediately fixed. It lasts for a couple of months and for others, it fluctuates over a long period of time. Hence there is a very special place for a sustaining ministry for these individuals even as they receive treatment through psychotherapy or antidepressants. The principle of *wu wei* can serve an important role in the sustaining ministry of pastoral care.

WU WEI *AND THE CYCLE OF DEPRESSION*

What is this principle of *wu wei? Wu wei* is about non-trying. Non-trying is not non-doing. Non-trying is about doing without trying. Trying here refers to the attempt of the self to seek affirmation of itself through the process of distinction (creating standards for comparison) and pursuing the goals based on this distinction (self-regulation) as an attempt to affirm the self. Through trying, one gets caught in its cycle. The principle of *wu wei,* in neutralizing the negating power of negativity, takes away discrepancy and therefore one need not try.

Positive Spiral of Recovery

Can one turn the downward slide around? If negativity activates depressive self-schema, and subsequent "trying" results in the self being caught within the cycle, since depressive self-schema negates every attempt to reduce discrepancy, how then can one exit this cycle?

Perhaps it is best to ask what leads to this "trying" process in the first place? We find both in the writings of Chuang Tzu and in self-regulatory perseveration theory the agreement that negativity leads one to question oneself. The self which is in doubt of its identity seeks affirmation through the process of "trying" or, in the language of self-regulatory perseveration, self-regulation. Underlying this movement toward "trying" is the basic question of self-worth. The self must have its worth. The self must have its meaning. It is only in the recognition of meaning and worth that the self can face mortality, vulnerability, and nonbeing. On the other hand, it is the lack of worth and meaning that leads one to enter episodes of depression that symbolize the death of the self. "The loss of self-esteem," writes Styron, "is a celebrated symptom, and my own sense of self had all but disappeared."[6] In describing the connection between depression and self-worth, Gotlib and Hammen write:

> Depression is thought to be a response to beliefs about self-worth and the inability to obtain self-worth validation. Individuals with preexisting dependency goals or dysfunctional self- and other-representations may be especially susceptible to interpersonal negative events; they may view them as depleting of personal value, and believe that the particular event cannot be repaired and that no alternative source of personal worth validation is available.[7]

It is, therefore, reasonable to claim that depressed individuals keep "trying" because they have not discovered their own worth and meaning. They are unable to exit this cycle of "trying" (although they keep persevering) because of their limited definition of self-worth, or, as Pyszczynski and Greenberg have pointed out, they get "stuck" because of the lack of an alternative route toward the acquisition of self-worth. Often a depressed person sees very few alternatives that can help to regain his or her self-worth. The scarcity of alternatives leads one to persist on trying to regain the lost object even with the awareness that achieving this standard is an unlikely possibility.[8]

If there is only one definition of self-worth then this must be pursued or the self will disintegrate, because to live without worth is to be worth nothing. How can this self find its worth and meaning? The fact that a person is getting depressed, argues Pyszczynski and Greenberg, is because this very source of worth that they keep pursuing is unattainable. Depression, as a form of resignation and hopelessness, is in a sense an invitation for depressed individuals to take a look at their source of worth because "this sense of resignation is the first step toward recovery. Only by realizing the impossibility of recovering the lost object can the individual begin the process of disengagement from the goal and reinvestment in alternative sources of self-worth."[9]

This concept is also reflected in the writing of Jungian psychologist David Rosen. Rosen suggests that the rate of suicide among depressed individuals suggests the experience of death of the self, which then results in suicide. In actuality, they do not want to kill the self. They want to kill their ego-image. The term ego-image here refers to their perception of themselves that they have acquired through the interaction between their inner self (psyche) and the external events and environment. It is this negative self-perception that has led to the experience of meaninglessness. This leads Rosen to name this therapeutic treatment ego-cide.[10]

This need to change the direction of one's effort in an attempt to attain an understanding of oneself is also reflected in the life of Kierkegaard. On August 16, 1847, Kierkegaard wrote in his journal:

> I feel now impelled to come to myself in a deeper sense, by coming closer to God in the understanding of myself. . . . I shall therefore keep quiet, not work too hard, yea, hardly at all, not begin a new book, but try to come to myself, to think thoroughly the thought of my melancholy together with God on this spot. In that way my melancholy may be relieved and Christianity come closer to me.[11]

According to self-regulatory perseveration theory, therapy for depression consists of assisting depressed individuals in the total subjection of themselves to the loss of self while at the same time providing a warm and accepting environment to minimize the effects of such loss. This approach aims at helping individuals realize that the "object is truly irretrievable and to fully experience the existential implications of this knowledge."[12] The next step is to help them see that there are other ways of acquiring self-worth, and that this process may call for the alteration of one's definition of self-worth. Further, since this definition is often located within one's worldview, it may even call for a radical shift in the understanding of one's worldview or reality. One's values, which are derived from one's cultural worldview, may be the factors that maintain one's definition of self-worth. Since core beliefs serve an important function in sustaining the sense of self, anything that undermines them can result in considerable distress for the client. Nevertheless, suggest Pyszczynski and Greenberg, this is exactly what is needed to reduce the client's vulnerability to future depressive episodes. If a client were to hold on to a view that has a negative impact on the psychological or physical well-being, it is the role of the therapist to help the client recognize the need for changes in the core beliefs.[13]

Wu Wei *As a Way Out*

How can this principle of *wu wei* help depressed individuals exit the cycle of depression? There are at least two important roles that *wu wei* can play in the alleviation of the negative experience of depression described by Pyszczynski and Greenberg. The first role is related to the problem of self-focused attention. The second role concerns the acquisition of alternative sources of self-worth as suggested by self-regulatory perseveration theory.

Self-Focused Attention

Self-focused attention activates negative self-schema that intensifies the symptoms of depression.[14] Shifting the focus away from the self, therefore, may lead to the alleviation of the depressive symptoms. Letting go of the lost object will enable one to withdraw from engaging in self-regulatory efforts, thus breaking the vicious cycle of negative affect, self-evaluation, and self-blame.[15] A study of the relationship of depression, self-focused attention, and negative memory bias by Edward J. Giaquinto Jr. concludes with similar suggestion that the negative memory bias may be reduced by teaching depressed individuals to focus their attention away from themselves.[16] Pyszczynski and Greenberg suggest the utilization of cognitive or behavioral therapy to distract the self from being self-focused.

> To the extent that the high level of self-focused attention inherent in self-regulatory perseveration on the lost object and the general-

ized depressive self-focusing style contribute to the continuing downward spiral of depression, reducing the individual's level of self-focus should produce a relatively rapid improvement in his or her outlook on life.[17]

How does *wu wei* deal with self-focused attention? Before we can arrive at this answer, I will review what *wu wei* states about self-worth, self-focus, discrepancy, self-regulation, self-perseveration, and the upward spiral. Although the language may differ, the ideas are rather similar in many respects.

When one becomes self-focused, one compares oneself with one's standards. To this, Chuang Tzu's advice is to empty yourself of all the contrasts through the process of reduction. When there are no standards with which to compare oneself, there is no discrepancy. When there is no awareness of the discrepancy, the self-focused attention is deactivated. Self-focused attention is deactivated because self-focused attention leads to comparison. When there is no comparison, there is no longer any need to focus on the self. Here is where *wu wei* differs from theories of self-focused attention. *Wu wei* does not seek to distract one from focusing the attention on oneself and thus *wu wei* is more realistic, more attuned to the reality of the human condition.

> The sage leans on the sun and moon, tucks the universe under his arm, merges himself with things, leaves the confusion and muddle as it is, and looks on slaves as exalted. Ordinary men strain and struggle; the sage is stupid and blockish. He takes part in ten thousand ages and achieves simplicity in oneness.[18]

According to the above passage, Chuang Tzu advises us to take away discrepancy all together. Without discrepancy, the need to try no longer exists. *Wu wei* removes the discrepancy through non-trying. This is a radical attitude. It is not achieved by trying to close the gap through the movement of the "is" toward the "ought." It is doing away with the "ought" and affirming the "is." Life realizes that what is, is good enough. It does not need to go elsewhere in search of affirmation. Where there is no comparison the self need not try. Where there are no contrasts, the "ought" and the "is" exist in one unity. The gap is closed not by trying but by non-trying; by emptying oneself from contrasts.

Chuang Tzu suggests "the fasting of the inner-self (commonly called 'the mind')" as a sage chides and admonishes a young zealot caught in the contrastive network of being and nothing. Mind-fasting is a discipline of mind-divesting, a divesting of those varied self-defeating passions for any single pole of the ontological contrasts in life. One vainly craves talents, sensory pleasures, emotions, knowledge, and morals, and one vainly strives to avoid their lack or their opposites. And yet one's lust traps one in much ado about nothing; the more one tries for these things, the farther away they are from one, and in the end one destroys oneself in futility. One must undo one's much ados and truly non-do and non-be.[19]

Alternative Source of Self-Worth

The second role of *wu wei* in dealing with the cycle of depression has to do with the acquisition of an alternative source of self-worth. According to Pyszczynski and Greenberg, one is caught in the downward spiral because one keeps pursuing the unattainable goal that defines one's self-worth. Because the self must have its worth, it keeps pursuing even when one recognizes the unattainability of this goal. According to this theory, the unattainability of the goal is not due to the lack of the ability of an individual, as much as the limited definition of the self (or the lack of an alternative source of self-worth). The cycle of "trying" is initiated in the pursuit of the self. With a limited definition of self-worth, one is unable to cease the process of "trying" because without "worth" the self has no meaning.

This is not the way to the self, suggests Chuang Tzu. The way to the self is not by trying to be what one thinks one ought to be. The "ought to be" is an imposition of cognition on the self. In describing this "trying" Stambaugh writes, "basically, there is nothing whatsoever we can 'do'; the doing is part of the problem, if not its source."[20] Trying to be in accord with one's logic is imposing rigid rules on life. It may be logical, but it is not life. Life transcends logic and cognition. The way to the self is by returning. To return is to deconstruct one's path of self-definition, to empty oneself of one's definition of worth and allow the self to emerge as is. To return is to move back to the self as is, with its *yin* and *yang*, good and bad, light and darkness. To return is to flow, which is

contradictory to the path of logic that discriminates. The way of returning suggests, in line with Pyszczynski and Greenberg, that an alternative
definition of self-worth is needed for one to move out of this cycle of
"trying."

What is this alternative source of self-worth? The "worth" of the
self is the worth of the "self" in itself. There is no need to go find the
self anywhere else. There is no need to try to acquire the worth. The
worth exists within the self itself. When the self finds the worth
within itself, the "ought" ceases to be. It ceases because the worth is
not found in the "ought." The striving for the "ought" that results in
self-regulatory perseveration and the cycle of depression is motivated
by the belief that the worth is in the "ought." But the philosophy of *wu
wei* suggests that the worth of the self is to be found in the very being of
this self. It is, and it is good enough. This is the alternative source of
self-worth as taught by Chuang Tzu and Lao Tzu. In *Tao Te Ching,* Lao
Tzu writes, "The Master never reaches for the great; thus she achieves
greatness."[21]

Among depressed individuals, the experience of negativity is being transformed by redefining worth. A depressed individual, whose
heightened self-awareness intensifies the experience of negativity
and whose every "trying" is being negated by the autonomic script of
self-blame, finds a resting place in non-trying or non-doing. This is so
because the worth is already there before one tries. When one's definition of "worth" excludes negativity, one is unable to rest in it.
Hence one has to strive, to overcome. But when "worth" is inclusive
of negativity itself, one does not need to strive. By redefining "worth"
from the perspective of *yin* and *yang,* one can rest in oneself. The affirmation exists and there is no cycle to exit. There is no cycle, because there is nothing to negate. There is nothing to negate, because
negativity has been embraced. Trying suggests that we are not good
enough and, hence, we need to try. Non-trying suggests that we are
good enough and, therefore, there is no need to try. All doing from
this point on becomes spontaneous. Actions become authentic. It becomes authentic because when the self does not have to strive to be
worth something, it can be anything. It can act in accord with its own
nature. When "worth" becomes an ontological quality within the
structure of finitude, the self is liberated. The self finally returns to it-

self not by trying but by non-trying. Hence it is not "worth the try" to find oneself. The "worth" is there a priori.

This practice of non-trying is made possible within the context of the Taoist understanding of the concept of nature. Nature is conceived not as an object to be analyzed, dissected, captured, and controlled. Nature is organic. Nature has a life of its own, and this includes human nature as well. Because nature has a life of its own, we can trust that nature will heal itself. Because nature has a life and a source of healing within itself, we can "sit down and do nothing," and things will still happen of their own accord. When I sit around and do nothing, the wind still blows, the grass still grows, the sun shines, the rain falls, the seed sprouts, and the cycle moves on. Even with the lack of a knowledge of anatomy and physiology, I still walk, talk, eat, and breathe. My heart still pumps and my brain is working. I do not know the mechanics of it. I know I am thinking, but I do not know how this thinking takes place. But it happens and so one can trust nature.

Speaking of the ability of nature to heal itself, Jung believes that something within our psyche directs us toward the wholeness of the self, something within that seeks to direct life.[22] It is this drive toward wholeness, as inherent in nature, that makes the practice of non-trying possible.

Summary

The processes of trying to fix oneself, affirm oneself, and perfect oneself and its cycle are often experienced by depressed individuals as an existential dread. People get tired of themselves. They feel sick thinking about themselves within this cycle of trying and non-trying. It is "sickness unto death" as described by Kierkegaard:

> So to be sick unto death is, not to be able to die-yet not as though there were hope of life; no, the hopelessness in this case is that even the last hope, death, is not available. . . . It is in this last sense that despair is the sickness unto death, this agonizing contradiction, this sickness in the self, everlastingly to die, to die and yet not to die the death. For dying means that it is all over, but dying the death means to live to experience death.[23]

In non-trying, the whole trying process ceases. The cycle does not exist. The self does not need to fix itself. The self does not need to try to affirm itself. The self becomes itself. It can become itself because it empties itself from all the "ought-to-be" imperatives, the "ought-to-be" that, in the very first place, places the self against itself and brings about contradiction within the self. Speaking of the "ought" in relation to contradiction, Bonhoeffer writes:

> For the Pharisee every moment of life becomes a situation of conflict in which he has to choose between good and evil. For the sake of avoiding any lapse his entire thought is strenuously devoted night and day to the anticipation of the whole immense range of possible conflicts, to the reaching of a decision in these conflicts, and to the determination of his own choice.[24]

Figure 8.1 illustrates the way negativity, through the process of self-evaluation, self-regulation, and negation, traps one in a cycle of depression. The crucial step in this process is the experience of negation, the perception of discrepancy, and intensified negative affects.

Here is where *wu wei* offers an exit point that reduces the intensity of negative affects. *Wu wei* invites us to flow along and not struggle. *Wu wei* invites us to embrace webbed toes instead of judging them from a psychosocial and scientific paradigm as abnormal. Depression is not something that we need to fight against, try to conquer, or get rid of. Depression is an expression of a psyche that seeks to direct the self toward wholeness. Depression is a language of the soul. Depression invites us to enter our soul and explore its depth. "For the soul," Moore suggests, "depression is an initiation, a rite of passage."[25] If we pathologize depression, it has no way to go but to be named abnormal, a "webbed toes" that needs curing. But, if we see it as an invitation, "[w]e might also discover that depression has its own angel, a guiding spirit whose job is to carry the soul away to its remote places where it finds unique insight and enjoys a special vision."[26] *Wu wei* does not ask us to resist but listen to the language of the soul as expressed through depression. It invites us to construct a perspective that is capable of including darkness and emptiness. It invites us to appreciate darkness that we may see light, emptiness that we may experience the meaning of fullness.

FIGURE 8.1. Cycle of Depression and *Wu Wei*

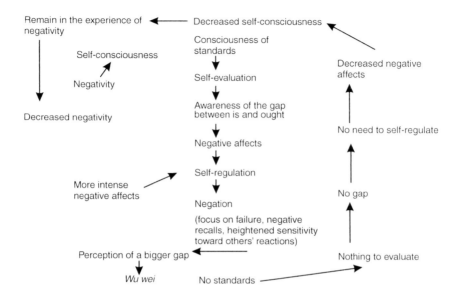

In its invitation for us to enter the stream and flow along in the pain of depression, it begs us to make full use of the force of gravity that resides in emptiness. When a space is filled, the flow ceases. The emptying process is particularly crucial to pastoral caregivers. Depressed individuals need to be encouraged to empty themselves of all the "ought to be" that they experience in excessive amounts. For Christians, the cross symbolizes their capability to empty the self of destructiveness. The cross symbolizes the power that not only takes away all the past *karma* but provides an affirmation of the self as it is. In the cross, the past is forgiven and the present is affirmed. The self need not try to affirm itself through the path that has been paved (the "ought to" and "ought not"). One is invited to believe in the power of the cross, and this belief or faith is affirmed through action that is performed on the basis of total freedom. Action is authentic only when one is totally free. This freedom is given us through Christ. In freedom there is no "ought to be," and there is no prescribed path. We must walk our own trail, pave our own path, and draw our own lines. But the principle of *wu wei* does not only help alleviate the pain caused by the negativity of depression. It speaks to the core issue of pastoral care which is the care of soul.

WU WEI *AND THE CARE OF THE SOUL*

The distress caused by the negativity of depression deposits a person in the midst of doubt regarding the meaning of the self. "What is the use of living when life is so painful?" is a common expression among depressed individuals. How can life be meaningful in the face of ongoing sadness and hopelessness? When anhedonia becomes a force that overwhelms one's life, the future is lost. Where is the meaning? This quest for meaning can be understood as a spiritual quest.[27] Spirituality addresses the question of meaning in the face of nonbeing. Therefore, we can also say that the struggle with depression is also the struggle with one's spirituality, because spirituality aims at making meaning of one's existence in the experience of nonbeing. It is a struggle to find worth in oneself when this self feels totally depleted. It is a struggle to find hope in the face of hopelessness. It is a struggle to find joy in the overwhelming experience of sadness. It is a struggle to find something that may make sense when the mind refuses to listen to reason. When the self is plunged into total chaos and insanity, the self searches desperately for a structure that one may be able to hold on to as a source of security.

Can there remain meaning in the experience of pain? Could it possibly be that perhaps pain actually emerges from the meaning we give to experience? In *Hanging On and Letting Go,* Pyszczynski and Greenberg argue that the problem depressed individuals face is the lack of alternative sources of definition for the self.[28] They both suggest that the source of self-definition is often found in one's cultural values including and sometimes especially religious values. Culture is built on worldview. Worldview is an expression of one's understanding of reality. This suggests that at some point, depressed individuals constructed an understanding of reality, consciously or unconsciously, and this constructed reality has been working against the self. The pain that the self is experiencing is a cry of the psyche seeking to inform the soul that, if there is to be meaning, there is a need to reconstruct the source of interpretation.

What is the source of interpretation or cultural worldview that serves to reinforce the depressive symptoms? Western culture seems to be living in a cultural worldview that is built on the philosophical concept of Being. We want Being. We are not totally fond of nonbeing. We like to look young and feel good. We want to be firm and slim. We hate it when our body parts begin to sag. We try to cover up our wrinkles.[29]

At the psychological level, too, we have been taught that the pursuit of happiness is the aim of life's journey. In describing this present age, Masao Abe, a Zen Buddhist, writes, "[T]he present age is one of fulfillment and enjoyment of life."[30] In such a pursuit, we scan shelves in bookstores searching for answers, and we find books such as *Stop Aging Now; Lean Bodies; Feeling Good: The New Mood Therapy; Being Happy;* and *Being Married Happily Forever.* It comes with no surprise that subjects in self-help sections of bookstores include "maximum sex" and "one-hour orgasm."

I personally have nothing against good sex, good mood, good marriage, and firm bodies. In fact I wish that my body were a lot firmer than it is right now. My problem is in defining reality purely from the perspective of being, while ignoring the nonbeing aspects of our lives. There is a consequence to this quest for being at the expense of nonbeing. Moore comments that "therapy sometimes emphasizes change so strongly that people often neglect their own natures and are tantalized by images of some ideal normality and health that may always be out of reach."[31] When we seek to change what is meant to be as an ontological quality of being, we are, in effect, changing for the worse. It is like trying to be human by ignoring human qualities within us.

> [M]odern psychology, perhaps because of its links to medicine, is often seen as a way of being saved from the very messes that most deeply mark human life as human. We want to sidestep negative moods and emotion, bad life choices and unhealthy habits. But if our purpose is first to observe the soul as it is, then we may have to discard the salvational wish and find deeper respect for what is actually there. By trying to avoid human mistakes and failures, we move beyond the reach of the soul.[32]

I believe this cultural worldview of Being makes it difficult for us to rest in the experience of negativity. When we fight against negativity, which is an ontological quality of our finitude, we fight against ourselves. We attempt to become wholistic by ignoring essential qualities of our beings. Watts writes, "[W]hat is ordinarily felt as the wayward, unpredictable, dangerous, and even hostile world—including one's capricious emotions and inner feelings—is actually one's own being and doing."[33]

This philosophical concept or cultural worldview of being plays a significant role in the way we deal with the negativity of depression. If we define Being as an "ought" that we must pursue and nonbeing as that which we need to overcome or avoid, then we set ourselves up for the pursuit of an unattainable goal without being able to cease this process. We cannot cease, because in every attempt, we experience the presence of negativity as an essential ontological quality of our finitude. The theology of nonbeing, on the other hand, allows us to rest because it sees negativity as a part of humanity. This is the theology that invites us to the "total acceptance of our human condition, of the real contingency in which we find ourselves" because, writes Raimundo Panikkar, "[T]o thirst is to transgress Reality, to evade the human situation."[34]

This theology calls depressed individuals to participate fully in the reality as it presents itself to us. "The reality in which vision begins and grows is life as we live it yesterday and today, the life that we live, touch, and feel, the life that gives us joy and hope, but also much, perhaps more sorrow and despair."[35] When we see nonbeing as a part of our reality, there is no longer a need to fight against it. When we embrace our shadow,[36] we stop fighting against ourselves and return to our souls.

Chapter 9

Wu Wei and the Practice
of Pastoral Care

A psychoneurosis must be understood, ultimately, as the suffering of a soul which has not discovered its meaning.

Carl Jung[1]

As discussed in previous chapters, the principle of *wu wei* helps a
person take the focus away from the self by undermining the discrepancy between "is" and "ought" and provides an alternative source of
worth and meaning by affirming the "is." At the spiritual level, it invites one to embrace nonbeing and, through embracing, enables one to
rest within oneself. The underlying principle that helps shift attention
away from the self, provide an alternative source of worth and meaning, and enable one to rest in oneself, is the embracing of negativity.
Through this process, negativity is depleted of its power to negate. It
deals with emptiness by emptying itself. How can these be applied to
the sustaining ministry of pastoral care?

I see five possible applications within the context of pastoral care.
First, pastoral caregivers can use *wu wei* to address the contexts (the
cultural and theological contexts that promote the pursuit of being at
the expense of nonbeing) that play a significant role in promoting the
distress of the souls. Second, pastoral caregivers can use *wu wei* to
walk with depressed people in their experience of negativity, without
trying to fix or get rid of depression but instead helping them find rest
in this experience. The third application of *wu wei* is its capacity to encourage depressed individuals to learn to trust in God or the process of
nature. Fourth, the principle of *wu wei* is useful for expanding the
meaning of what is normative. Fifth, *wu wei* can be used on a one-to-one

basis that will help depressed individuals explore their issues in greater depth.

ADDRESSING THE CONTEXT

The context that promotes distress of the soul can be addressed by pastoral caregivers through preaching, teaching, and other symbolic means. In addressing the spiritual struggle of depressed individuals, there is a need to articulate the concept of nonbeing as an existential ontological quality of our finitude. Life is not about the pursuit of Being. Life is not about getting rid of pain, illness, and death. Life is about living in the midst of birth and death. Abe writes:

> Through objectification we cling to life and hate death. We are shackled by the opposition between life and death. Nevertheless, we are always confronted by death through the very fact that we are alive. Life and death are as inseparable as two sides of a sheet of paper. Nor is this an ordinary sheet of paper upon which we may idly gaze. We are this sheet of paper with its two sides of life and death. Therefore, at any moment of our life we are all life and all death. Our life is not a movement from life towards death, but a continual living-dying, a paradoxical and dynamic oneness of life and death.[2]

The concept of nonbeing is directly related to the concept of finitude. As pastoral caregivers, therefore, we need to educate those in our care to be faithful to God by recognizing their creatureliness. This process also includes the need to empty ourselves of the image of God we have created. Speaking of this process of emptying, Richard Rohr states, "[T]he journey of faith demands that we let go of our image of God and our image of ourselves. But we can't do that in our head or on our own; it's done to us. The only thing we have to do is live, but live openly and honestly and let the truth of the world get to us."[3]

This emptying process should also lead to the evaluation of our value system. Often our values are inherited from our cultural worldview at the unconscious level. In Western culture we are worth something if we are successful, attractive, wealthy, healthy, smart, and have social grace. But as human beings, are these the basis of our worth? Reflecting on the meaning of spirituality and the Western culture, Rohr writes:

> Meister Eckhart said that the spiritual life has more to do with subtraction than with addition. But in the capitalistic West here's what we've done with the Gospel: We keep climbing high up the ladder of spiritual success, and we've turned the Gospel into a matter of addition instead of subtraction.[4]

We hear a similar concern from Lao Tzu:

> For every step forward a step or two back.
> To such laughters a level road looks steep,
> Top seems bottom,
> White appears black,
> Enough is a lack,
> Endurance is a weakness,
> Simplicity a faded flower.
> But eternity is his who goes straight round the circle,
> Foundation is his who can feel beyond touch,
> Harmony is his who can hear beyond sound,
> Pattern is his who can see beyond shape:
> Life is his who can tell beyond words
> Fulfillment of the unfulfilled. [5]

The culture that pursues Being is indeed reflecting the inner depletion within itself. The worth has to be acquired because of the lack of recognition of the self's intrinsic value. Rohr further states, "[I]f we haven't lived and experienced enough within ourselves, we're tempted to accumulate more and more outer things as substitutes for self-worth." What we really need to recognize is, affirms Rohr, "we needn't acquire what we already have."[6]

WALKING WITH DEPRESSED INDIVIDUALS

Pastoral caregivers can walk with depressed individuals in their pain. Caring is not curing. "Care of the soul," states Moore, "is not solving the puzzle of life . . . it is an appreciation of the paradoxical mysteries that blend light and darkness into the grandeur of what human life and culture can be."[7] Similarly Rohr affirms, "The soul can't be fixed. It just is."[8] The act of walking with and not trying to fix the negativity of depression speaks symbolically of the art of letting go. When we acknowledge another's pain without trying to take it away, we allow individuals to look into their own pain and negativity. This symbolic act conveys the recognition of pain as an ontological structure of human finitude. We all must endure pain. It is inescapable. Pain is manageable when we know that someone cares. Pain is tolerable when we know that we are loved.

How then can we walk with depressed individuals by using the principle of *wu wei?* The experience of negativity is often expressed through negative memory bias, negative self-perception, self-blame, and self-negation. As has been stated earlier, this experience leads depressed individuals to try to affirm themselves. Depressed individuals may try to overcome the pain of depression by obsessively analyzing why they feel the way they feel in order to hypothesize the cause. They may try to change the way they think about themselves in order to feel better about themselves, or they may try to consciously behave differently in a social setting to align themselves with the standards of social norms. They may even try to force themselves to behave in a certain way in order to feel normal. In this whole process, they experience a heightened awareness of themselves as an object (objective self-consciousness). In all these attempts, they keep moving farther and farther away from themselves, from the way they feel or the way they normally behave to what they think they should feel, think, or behave.

The *wu wei* approach does not encourage depressed individuals to try to change their thinking or behavior, but to sit in the discomfort of their thinking, feeling, and behavior. Non-trying suggests that there is no goal for the self to try to attain. It is an art of learning to sit in what one perceives as obsessive thinking, negative feeling, and dysfunctional behavior allowing oneself to experience the full spectrum of these processes without any judgment. The principle of *wu wei* does not encourage depressed individuals to try to change their thinking or behavior. It does not analyze nor seek to explain the experience of negativity. Here depressed individuals are asked to remain in the experience of negativity without trying to analyze, trying to improve, trying to change themselves, or trying to explain their experience of negativity. To try to analyze or improve presupposes rational constructs of what it means to be healthy emotionally, what it means to behave within the social norm, or what it means to have worth in oneself. To try presupposes theological and philosophical constructs. Psychotherapists Greg Johanson and Ron Kurtz, who have been influenced by Taoist and Buddhist philosophy, express a similar concern.

> [I]t is not helpful to pour out theories, explanations, illustrations, justifications, and stories on top of stories. This tends to engage our minds alone, which are often already overloaded, defended, and ruled by habitual responses. Analyzing and talking about our lives, as if giving a report about past events, does not encourage contact with our core. Our core is that central, usually unconscious place within us that controls how we experience events by filtering what comes to us through previously constructed beliefs about life.[9]

They both suggest that the way to reach our core is through "emptying our minds of theories and turning our awareness inward toward present experience."[10] This is what the non-trying method is about—a movement toward emptying one's constructs of reality upon which one comes to perceive one's worth as an individual. The pastoral role within this context is to encourage depressed individuals to respond to the experience of negativity by practicing non-trying. When the experience of negativity evokes the urge to try to close the gap between what is and what one "ought to be" (socially acceptable, emotionally healthy, or successful as defined by one's culture), depressed individuals are encouraged not to try to fix themselves whether it be through analysis, comparison, improvement, judgment of negativity, or change of behavior. They are encouraged to befriend "the uneasiness-not trying to change it in any way, allowing it to emerge more fully."[11] While learning to sit in the experience of negativity, they need to go about doing their normal day-to-day duties within the limits of their ability, doing what they can do, and not judging themselves for what they cannot do.

Caution needs to be exercised when ministering to depressed persons who are suicidal. Pastoral caregivers need to be aware of the risk of suicide in relation to depression. It is estimated that more than 60 percent of people who commit suicide suffer from depression.[12] When these people are suicidal, the non-doing approach can be used as an excuse in favor of their suicidal inclination. A more directive approach to this type of situation is needed and perhaps this is not the place to encourage the practice of *wu wei*.[13]

ENCOURAGING TRUST

This third function has a very significant theological implication. James Hillman inquires, "[W]hy is it so difficult to imagine that I am cared about, that something takes an interest in what I do, that I am perhaps protected, maybe even kept alive not altogether by my own will and doing?"[14] Chuang Tzu teaches that while we sit down and do nothing, the rain falls and the tree grows. Nature is organic. In theological language, we say that God is active in our lives. God is also active in the healing process. We can trust that the healing will come. In affirming this point, Johanson and Kurtz write that "[W]hen something is developing organically, the next right action inevitably suggests itself, as does the right rhythm for acting. Much of therapy is an act of trust. When things seem muddy, we can be patient if we believe they will eventually become clear."[15] Edwin Friedman, a pastoral counselor and a rabbi, shares a similar view. Friedman believes we can have faith in the natural process and trust that the healing will come because "life moves toward life. In other words, life does not have to be taught how to do it."[16]

This practice of trust can be encouraged by discouraging depressed individuals from the inclination to fix themselves through the process of analysis, and encouraging them to allow the experience to take its course and reflect on this course at a later time. It can also be encouraged through meditating on scriptural passages such as Psalms 23. Meditation is often used in Eastern religions as a method of emptying and remaining centered in oneself. Meditation can, therefore, enhance the emptying process which is crucial to the principle of *wu wei*. Selected scriptural passages provide contents for meditation that encourage trust. While *wu wei* speaks of nature as a source of healing, biblical passages speak of God who is fully engaged in this healing process. Before entering this passage, pastoral caregivers invite depressed individuals to sit up straight, slowly take a deep breath, and exhale. Repeat this process five to six times. Open the Scripture to the selected passages. Read the passages slowly. Meditate on the passages while practicing deep breathing.[17]

EXPANDING THE MEANING OF NORMATIVE

The fourth application deals with the expansion of the theological assumption regarding what is normative. Chuang Tzu writes:

> Thus a web between the toes is but the addition of a useless piece of flesh and an appendage on a hand is but the implanting of a useless finger. One who adds webs and appendages to the attributes of the five viscera, so that they are debauched and perverted by humane and righteous conduct, is to be meddlesome in the use of keen hearing and eyesight.[18]

A pastoral caregiver who is filled with theories on psychopathology and whose definition of mental health excludes the experience of depression will not be able to allow depressed individuals to sit in the experience of negativity. Speaking of the tendency toward pathology in this society, Hillman warns:

> The vicious inadequacy of treatment is not intended by practitioners, who mean well. It results willy-nilly from the inadequacy, or viciousness, of theory. So long as the statistics of normalizing developmental psychology determine the standards against which the extraordinary complexities of a life are judged, deviations become deviants. Diagnosis coupled with statistics is the disease.[19]

A pathologized depression results in an attempt to remove its negativity, which leads to the negating process that traps depressed individuals in its cycle. The expansion of the meaning of what is normative can permit depressed individuals to come to the realization that depression may not always be pathological. It may also be the voice of our psyche begging us to pay attention to our soul. In summary, the application of the principle of *wu wei* to the sustaining ministry of pastoral care is well captured by Johanson and Kurtz. In describing the function of therapists, they write: "Our process often develops with minimal need for guidance. The master therapist is always noted for how little he does."[20]

ONE-TO-ONE

Goal

The goal of this *wu wei* intervention in pastoral counseling is to reduce the potential of the negativity of depression to negate the self and draw this self into the cycle of trying.

Objectives

1. To assess the level of depression and identify standards whereby one employs to judge oneself

2. To educate depressed individuals of the diagnosis, epidemiology, possible recurrence, psychological theories of depression, biological basis of depression, and psychotropic medication

3. To create awareness of the standards one sets for oneself in different settings

4. To empty oneself of the standards one uses to judge oneself

5. To explore spirituality as an alternative source of healing

Assessment

The assessment will deal with two factors. First will be an assessment of the level of depression using Beck's Depressive Inventory. This assessment will be useful in determining the level of depression (mild, moderate, and severe). A severe case should be referred to other professionals.

The second factor will deal with the assessment of negativity. In religious terms, it is an assessment of an individual's guilt. One needs to keep in mind that negativity here refers to the self's ability to negate itself and that this negation negates one's attempt at affirming one's self. Hence in assessing the negativity one has to address the experience of conflicts brought about by the inability of the self to fulfill one's goals. The assessment of negativity can be approached through asking depressed individuals to identify the experience of conflicts and the relation of conflicts to what one believes one ought to be. Questions that can aid in this process are:

1. What triggers the experience of conflict within you?

2. Do you see yourself as a perfectionist?

3. What often brings about self-blame?

4. What are some of the standards you set for yourself?

5. What can trigger you into a cycle of obsessive thinking?

6. What often leads you to feel bad about yourself?

The aim in this second assessment is to identify the "ought" that brings about the experience of conflicts within oneself. Another way to achieve this is to ask depressed individuals to become aware and to identify the standards which one uses to judge oneself and one's performance. The assessment process should also provide a space for depressed individuals to articulate the "madness" of depression that cannot be articulated elsewhere for fear of being misunderstood. Pastoral counselors should encourage the expression of feelings using guiding questions that relate to depressive illness.

Education

An educational process is an important aspect in the treatment of depression in that it provides depressed individuals with an understanding of what the self is going through at the psychological and biological level. Understanding empowers because it gives the feeling of control, at a certain level, of oneself. This psychoeducational process should include understanding of epidemiology of depression, the length of depression, the relationship between depression and social interaction, possible recurrent, psychological theories of depression, biological explanation of depression, and psychotropic medication.

Awareness

Often people who are depressed may not be able to identify the "ought-to-be" scripts that they use in a day-to-day operation. Pastoral caregivers need to encourage these individuals to be more aware by giving examples of how one judges oneself and sets standards for oneself in a variety of settings. The different types of awareness that can be helpful to identify are: awareness of one's standards in different settings and awareness of one's interpretation of stimuli.

Awareness of One's Standards

Depressed individuals need to become aware of how they consciously and unconsciously tell themselves how they should behave under different circumstances. They may tell themselves that they should be talkative, cheerful, or funny in a social setting, and that they should receive very high scores in their studies. Through practice in actual day-to-day operation they will be able to identify more "oughts" that play a role in intensifying conflicts within themselves.

Awareness of One's Interpretation of Stimuli

Depressed individuals get into the habit of interpretation without realizing that interpretation is not a fact. For example, when Mr. A notices that his friend lacks a warm expression on her face during their conversation, Mr. A's normal depressive response is to interpret his friend's action in the negative. "She did not like me." "I should not have said that to her." This process of interpretation is marked by one's bias toward negativity and hence, is not often in the service of the self.

Emptiness

Chuang Tzu teaches that the way to overcome the split between the reflexive self and the empirical self is through the process of reduction, or emptying oneself. Emptiness aims at reducing the prescribed path given to oneself, the standards one sets in order to judge oneself. I suggest two stages in achieving emptiness: meditation and reduction.

Meditation

The first stage of emptiness is reduction through meditation. The meditation process starts with breathing exercises, followed by the process of quieting oneself. This second process aims at becoming aware of one's standards, other's projection, and one's interpretation. The step in meditation is the mental removal of the three awarenesses. Pastors can assist depressed individuals by helping them to name the three awarenesses in concrete situations so that the meditative process can be directed at these concrete situations in which one sets standards, allows other's projections to disrupt oneself, and interprets stimuli that intensifies negativity.

Reduction

The second stage of emptiness involves the practice of emptiness or reduction within the context itself. In the awareness of the circumstances that trigger the inclination to set standards, whereby one judges oneself, one learns to practice the process of reduction when facing or anticipating the triggers.

Spirituality

Perhaps one of the greatest strengths of the principle of *wu wei* is its emphasis on spirituality. Spirituality here refers to the need for meaning in the face of nonbeing. It is easy to find meaning when we are in comfort or when life is going well. It is easy to speak of meaning in terms of light, joy, happiness, success, strength, and health. This is meaning in "Being." But how do we find meaning when we face death, pain, weakness, abandonment, sadness, conflict, and darkness? This is the realm of nonbeing. There is a need to arrive at meaning in the face of nonbeing. How can one arrive at meaning in the face of nonbeing? This is where the spiritual journey starts. Spirituality is the art of making meaning at the existential level. It is participative and experiential. I suggest four movements in pursuing a spiritual journey: embracing nonbeing, embracing shadows, embracing mystery, and "sitting down and doing nothing."

Embracing Nonbeing

This movement involves one's existential ability to recognize one's weaknesses and pain and to arrive at a place where it is all right to be weak and to experience pain. The individual can start by examining aspects of life in which he or she is unable to achieve goals and, through the understanding of grace, recognize that he or she is being embraced by God even in failure and sin. The next step in embracing nonbeing is to see that even in weaknesses and failures one still has the ability to contribute to others. The person may come to see that life is not about being perfect or sinless. Life is not about being the best, but that, even in the midst of pain and weaknesses one remains capable of touching lives and contributing positive influence to others.

Embracing Shadows

This process acquires a significant meaning for depressed individuals. The high level of guilt reflects a high level of "ought." This high level of "ought" in turn suggests the inability of the self to embrace within itself its shadows. For pastoral caregivers, it is important that grace be clearly understood because it is through the Cross that one can face one's shadow. It is the Cross that makes possible the ability to look into oneself and embrace that darkness. This is an essential step because, as Jung suggests, the psyche always moves toward wholeness. The shadow that is denied will emerge elsewhere. In this case, the shadow is being expressed through depressive symptoms, through the negativity that keeps negating the self. By embracing this shadow we can deny that very force of negation itself and return the self to its wholeness.

The formation of the personal shadow begins in very early childhood through interaction with parents and significant others in the immediate environment. Negative parental reactions toward a child's natural instincts can impair capacity for later expression in adult life. Children who are required to be nice and good and never be seen as dirty, bad, or angry, learn very early that to survive in society they need to present only the positive sides and repress the instinctive urges. Very soon these children learn to hide these feelings from themselves as well. Much of the personal shadow has been formed by the age of six or seven. This takes place not by what parents say, but how they behave and relate to the child.

Shadow has a significant value and psychic energy. When it is unrecognized it can be destructive to the soul. When it is recognized it proves to be a gold mine. For this reason it is important for us to confront our shadow. Confronting our shadow is the first task in the process of individuation. We confront our shadow by first experiencing it through our projection upon an object outside of us. This will, hopefully, lead to our ability to distinguish between ourselves and our shadow. The ability to distinguish will result in the ability to maintain an objective attitude toward our own personality.

We project onto others that which we are not able to integrate or come to terms with in ourselves. So the tension that we cannot stand within ourselves manifests itself in the form of psychic tension and relational problems. In Jung's perspective, the challenge is for us to learn to withdraw our projections upon others and deal with the shadow ourselves.

Embracing Mystery

This movement aims at recognizing the finite factor of our rationality. God is beyond and, therefore, one needs to see that our rationality is limited by our finiteness. We cannot capture God and hope that God will work along a certain logic. God has His own way of doing things. We need to let God be God and remain human in our understanding. Life cannot be neatly defined. The embracing of the mystery of God is a recognition of Buddha's silence and his smile. It is, as Bonhoeffer suggests, creatures remaining creatures. It is not imposing the "how" to the Christological question but the "who." Who is this Christ who transcends my Logos? This question is asked on the assumption that the Logos can comprehend the Logos and not vice versa. This is an essential theological journey in the healing process.

Sitting Down and Doing Nothing

The final aim of all religions is liberation. From a *wu wei* perspective, the ultimate liberation comes when one can learn to sit down and do nothing. By sitting down and doing nothing, the Chinese sages had in mind the ability to trust. To trust is to believe that nature has its own course. In Christian perspective, to trust is to believe that God will take care of us and hence we can let go. Letting go means allowing ourselves to believe that God or nature is in control. The art of letting go involves the ability to stay with whatever comes our way.

In the case of depression, it is the ability to stay with the experience of negativity. When one experiences the lack of self-confidence or emotional conflicts, letting go is to remain with the experience without attempting to judge the experience as good or bad. It is not judging the experience as bad and therefore trying to fix the problem. But it is not seeing it as a problem and learning to remain in that experience. It is, while experiencing the negativity, to be able to say "This is me and it is all right." It is all right because one comes to see oneself as a part of nature, a part of God, and one learns to believe that God heals. The problem starts when one tries to fix oneself because, in the attempt at fixing oneself, one interferes with nature's course. Hence the ability to sit down and do nothing must be built on the belief and trust in nature or God.

This concept is similar to Bowen's understanding that nature heals. He proposes that life always moves toward life, and, therefore, it does not have to be taught how. Maturation has its own time. It will always move in its own course. One cannot hurry this process and often, pain may be an essential ingredient in this maturation process. In describing this healing process, Edwin Friedman writes:

> The healer, in other words, does not have to take responsibility for making health happen, but for discovering the universal forces that make life tick, and then lining up the client's thinking and functioning with those life-sustaining forces that have continuously evolved since Creation. One may, therefore, have "faith" in natural processes.[21]

In learning to sit down and do nothing one moves along in the flow of gravity. To move along smoothly one needs to learn to not tell life how it should be. One needs to learn to stop telling life what being is all about. When we try to tell life how it should be, we block the flow of our psyche because life is not a set of logic that can be predicted through cognitive calculation. Feeling has its own logic and the heart has its own mind. Psyche understands the language of the soul. It is through the flow that we may find our souls. Souls speak and our task is to listen and not to dictate.

Chapter 10

Wu Wei and the Theology
of Pastoral Care

I was especially impressed with those who spoke of their depression as a gift from which they had learned valuable lessons.
While I could not relate emotionally or intellectually with vi-
sions of reincarnation or explanations of depression as central to
a God-given life mission, I left many interviews with a sense
that spiritually engaged individuals were in touch with something important.

David Karp[1]

Is there a theological basis for the use of the principle of *wu wei* in
the practice of pastoral care? As pastoral caregivers and counselors
we are concerned with the theological basis that informs our practice.
This is especially so when a foreign principle such as the principle of
wu wei is being incorporated into the practice of pastoral care. Can
pastoral caregivers adopt a principle based on Taoist philosophy?
How can we use a non-Christian principle in our ministry to fellow
Christians? Are we not betraying our faith?

I would like to address these questions by looking at the concept of
nonbeing. What is nonbeing and is this concept compatible with
Christian theology? If it is, what is the relationship between *wu wei*
and nonbeing and why it can be applied to the practice of pastoral
care? What are the ethics or moral implications of this principle if we
are encouraged to move beyond defining "standards"?

Before pursuing the clarification of the concept of nonbeing in Christian theology I would like to make two comments regarding the principle

of *wu wei*. First, the teaching of Lao Tzu and Chuang Tzu is not prescriptive but evocative. It does not provide an answer, but it evokes in us that need to find an answer for ourselves. By engaging in this process we authenticate ourselves. Therefore, although the teaching of *wu wei* may rest on another religious tradition, its aim is not to place a person in any particular religious tradition but to aid that person in walking the spiritual journey that each must walk by himself or herself.

Second, a basic difference is evident in the usage of the term nonbeing in Lao Tzu and Chuang Tzu and in Christian theology. To Lao Tzu and Chuang Tzu, nonbeing is the basis of "being and becoming." Nonbeing, therefore, is a metaphysical reality. In Christianity, "Being" is prior to nonbeing. What is intended in this book is the utilization of the term "nonbeing" at the ontological level and not metaphysical. By so doing, the application of this principle becomes existential which does not require an alteration of one's worldview. I see nonbeing as an essential part of human reality while believing that Being precedes nonbeing taking into consideration the Christian concept of the "fall."

NONBEING

What is nonbeing? I have been fascinated with the concept of nonbeing for a number of years. When I was first introduced to the concept through the writings of Paul Tillich and Martin Heidegger, I did not quite understand the meaning of nonbeing, but I found myself being attracted to this concept. Even now I do not know for certain if I really understand it. Nevertheless, it has become more and more important as I ponder on its meaning. I was not only attracted to the concept of nonbeing, I found it profound, even in my experience during my Clinical Pastoral Education internship. Reflecting on my clinical experience, I wrote:

> The sharing of brokenness makes me think of a theological concept of nonbeing. Being is finite. Time is temporal. Space is limited. Pain and suffering remind one of one's nonbeing, of one's finiteness. We are like grass in the field. The acceptance of nonbeing is encountering Being. To face the finiteness of our being is to come face to face with God, is to question the Being

as the ground of our very "being." Hence to face nonbeing, in essence, is an invitation to spirituality. In experiencing our brokenness, life speaks to us. Life tells us that there is another dimension to reality. Life tells us that in our brokenness, time is being confronted by eternity. Life tells us that "being" is not ultimately "nonbeing" but "Being." Death is an invitation to life. It is in the face of death that one is awaken to the deeper meaning of "life." The stories of brokenness were to me, invitations to life, to a greater participation of life.[2]

In the West, the concept of nonbeing has been developed from the ancient Greek language. Plato uses the concept to bring about contrast between existence and pure essence. Aristotle implies it in his distinction between matter and form. Augustine employs it in his interpretation of the concept of sin. Hegel sees the necessity of nonbeing or negation in the process of dialectic. It is also present in processed thought because it makes becoming possible. In existentialism, Heidegger places nonbeing at the core of his ontology. It is the awareness of nonbeing that evokes in a person the need to authenticate oneself.[3]

The concept of nonbeing in the East is expressed through the writings of Lao Tzu and Chuang Tzu. In discussing Chuang Tzu's theory of nonbeing, Wu sees it as a necessary epistemological basis of being since one can know what is only on the basis of what is not. It is also prior ontologically because being emerges from nonbeing.[4] According to Wang Pi, a neo-Taoist who lived around the third century, nonbeing is beyond name and form. It is the ultimate reality itself. Similarly the *Book of Changes* recognizes nonbeing as the underlying factor that unites all phenomena.[5] How does it unite all phenomena? The phenomena here include light and darkness, good and evil, speech and silence, softness and firmness, black and white. It unites by allowing the opposing factors to remain together in one unity. This is possible through emptiness. It empties itself of all preconceived ideas. It rids itself of logic. Logic disunifies. Logic places light and darkness in tension. Emptiness unites. Lao Tzu writes:

> Thirty spokes are made one by holes in a hub
> By vacancies joining them for a wheel's use;
> The use of clay in moulding pitchers
> Comes from the hollow of its absence;

Doors, windows, in a house,
Are used for their emptiness:
Thus we are helped by what is not
To use what is.

We join spokes together in a wheel,
but it is the center hole
that makes the wagon move.

We shape clay into a pot,
but it is the emptiness inside
that holds whatever we want.

We hammer wood for a house,
but it is the inner space
that makes it livable.

We work with being,
but nonbeing is what we use.[6]

In concrete practical human terms emptiness refers to the ability to empty ourselves of the tendency to create tension within the self through self-definition, through the desire to create distinction. To define something as "good" is to suggest the existence of "bad." Once we define something as "bad," this "bad" becomes, existentially, undesirable. The undesirable is to be avoided or overcome. Hence the self that is filled with logic, definition, and distinction is unable to hold the tension. It must get rid of the undesirable. But the emptied self is able to hold that which "is" together without trying to impose distinction on reality itself. The emptied self sees reality as it is. It does not categorize pain as bad and pleasure as good. It sees joy in tears and sorrow in happiness. It unites the tension and allows the things that seem, logically, diametrically opposed to coexist.[7] In describing the relationship between *yin* and *yang,* Jung Young Lee states:

Two opposites are not in conflict but are understood to complement each other. In conflicting dualism, we must fight our opposite and win by eliminating it. This kind of dualistic thinking is a pervasive form of an either/or thinking that represents the Western mind. However, in complementary dualism, we must not fight our opposite, because the opposite is essentially part of ourselves. In this respect, the elimination of the opposite is none other than the elimination of ourselves.[8]

Nonbeing, in my estimation, is finitude. It is the possibility of illness, pain, sorrow, and death that can evoke a sense of insecurity. The need for security can lead us to try to overcome our weakness, to accumulate for fear of poverty, to achieve for fear of failure, to gain for fear of loss, to seek approval for fear of rejection. Ultimately, this insecurity is the result of the threat of nonbeing, the possibility that we may not "be" both existentially and psychologically. [9] But the truth is we are finite human beings. We will die. We will get sick. We will get hurt. We do have needs. We get hungry. We have sexual desire. We want love. These factors make us human beings. They are a part of us. They are a part of our finiteness.[10] Nonbeing is a part of us whether we like it or not.

Nonbeing and Wu Wei

What is the relationship between nonbeing and *wu wei?* I believe that, as finite human beings, it is not possible to rest if we do not embrace nonbeing. If we persist in trying to overcome, eliminate, and avoid the qualities of nonbeing within us, life will be filled with an unending process of striving.

Perhaps the best place to start exploring the connection between nonbeing and *wu wei* is Heidegger's concepts of being and time. According to Heidegger, human beings find themselves as already being there in the world.[11] The awareness of the self as being in the world also raises an awareness of the contingency of being. The contingency of being lies in the fact that this being is being toward death. Humans realize that they are moving toward nothingness. In this movement, humans can get caught in the inauthenticity of life when they are distracted and disturbed by everyday cares, things, and people surrounding them. The way toward authenticity of life in the face of nonbeing is to strive for Being through conscience. The way toward Being is through striving for the "ought" in the face of nothingness as a way of self-affirmation.[12] In summarizing Heidegger's *Being and Time,* Grene writes, "[T]he dominant theme of Being and Time remains the vision of the lonely will driven by dread to face the prospect of its own dissolution, in retrospect its guilt, and yet to realize in this twin terror its proper freedom."[13]

In this analysis one recognizes the primacy of Being over nonbeing. Heidegger was searching for Being and this search is initiated by the awareness of nonbeing, of death. Here, to find Being is to overcome nonbeing. When one defines life in terms of being one is unable to rest because the qualities of nonbeing keeps emerging. One wonders if the quest for Being is the only path to authentic life. Perhaps for this very same reason, Heidegger's understanding of Being, as expressed in his later writings, includes nothingness.[14]

This description of Heidegger's thoughts illustrates the relationship between nonbeing and *wu wei*. When life is defined in terms of Being, nonbeing must be overcome or eliminated. We cannot aim at achieving Being. To try to do so implies the continual struggle for unactualizable goals. The reality of the self is the coexistence of being and nonbeing. In embracing nonbeing one is able to rest. In accepting nonbeing one can practice non-trying, *wu wei*.

NONBEING AND PASTORAL THEOLOGY

The concept of nonbeing has been expressed by a number of theologians. Due to the limited space, I wish to discuss the concept of nonbeing in the writings of Paul Tillich and Dietrich Bonhoeffer.

Paul Tillich

To Tillich, finitude forms the basis for the transition from essential being to existential being. This is so because the basis of human finitude lies in the fact that human beings are limited by nonbeing. Humans are the only beings that can experience the "shock of nonbeing," envisage nothingness, and ask the ontological question about the mystery of Being and nonbeing. Within this movement their ability to imagine infinity makes them sharply aware of their finitude. This self-awareness of the finite self produces anxiety. Anxiety is the fundamental quality of humans. It is the inward expression of the outward finitude.

Following in the tradition of Heidegger and Kierkegaard, Tillich makes a clear distinction between fear and anxiety. Fear has a specific object but in anxiety there is no specific object. If there is to be an object for anxiety that object is "nothingness." Ontological anxiety is beyond the power of psychotherapy to remove since it is occasioned by the unchangeable structure of human finitude. This point is significant to the practice of pastoral care and counseling. It is not the aim of pastoral care and counseling to remove ontological anxiety. To try to remove this anxiety is to attempt the restructuring of human finitude. The aim is to befriend this anxiety and embrace our finitude.[15]

In concrete practical terms, the categories through which finitude is manifested are time, space, causality, and substance. These categories are present in everything since everything participates in being and nonbeing.

Time

The negative aspect of time is its transitoriness. The positive aspect of time is that the temporal process is creative. The tension of time is expressed through the anxiety of transitoriness and the courage of a self-affirming present. Here Tillich points to the fact that time makes us aware of our nonbeing. But this can be balanced through the courage to affirm the present, the affirmation of temporality that gives human beings the power to resist the annihilating character of time.

Space

Every being must have space (home, place, city, country, and social space). When space is given, Being is affirmed. The negative aspect of space is that since being is finite, space is limited. Through nonbeing, Being loses every possible space. The anxiety of space is expressed through insecurity. Through this anxiety we strive to create a space in the social and political system. This space can be affirmed through the courageous recognition that this space is our as long as life still remains.

Causality

To cause is to lead to an existence of that which is caused. Negatively, to be caused is to not have the power of being in itself. Contingency is the character of Being. But this awareness may be balanced by a courage that accepts this negativity and seeks to achieve a kind of self-reliance. This takes place when we learn to be dependent even when structurally speaking we are interdependence.

Substance

The positive aspect of substance is self-identity. The negative side is the reverse of the positive in that this self-identity is nothing but an accident. The identity that is derived from the given substance is an accident. The nonbeing characteristic of substance may be affirmed through creativity, love relationships, and other acts in concrete situations.

Tillich helps us understand the place of nonbeing as an ontological reality in which we all participate. Here the Cross symbolizes the courage to accept the reality of finitude in the quest for meaning. The courage to embrace our finitude is the courage to create meaning even in the face of nonbeing.

Dietrich Bonhoeffer

Bonhoeffer's concept of nonbeing is expressed through the term creatureliness. Human beings are creatures and not the Creator. Hence we need to acknowledge our creatureliness. Bonhoeffer affirms a great danger in the creature losing sight of his creatureliness. Human beings, as creatures, are being thrown into the middle of time. From this middle we cannot know where we are heading unless we know our beginning. From the middle we can realize our direction only when we know our beginning. If we try to direct our own path without knowing our beginning, we will go against the structure of our being and end in alienation. The creature must learn to live as a creature, in obedience to God's word. When the creature seeks to define the knowledge of good and evil, the nature of God, and one's destiny through self-reflection, one is actually acting as the Creator. Only the Creator knows what is good and evil. Our inability to ordain our own path results from the fact that we can know our essence from our Creator. This is the limit of creatures. We are limited by the fact that we cannot ordain our own path without going against the structure of our beings, our essence.

> Adam's life comes from the middle which is not Adam himself but God. It constantly revolves around this middle without ever making the attempt to make this middle of existence its own possession. It is characteristic of man that his life is a constant circling around its middle, but that it never takes possession of

it. And this life from the middle, which only God possesses, is undisturbed as long as man does not allow himself to be flung out of his groove.[16]

Because of the necessity to accept our creatureliness, our limits, God, through grace, created the tree of the knowledge of good and evil. It is grace because through this tree God teaches human beings the need for the realization of their limits. Our limitation is the gift of life. This life will belong to us as long as we acknowledge this limitation. In this tree God confronts Adam and points out his limits. Through the prohibition of this tree God tells Adam that he is free. But through the prohibition of this tree God also makes known to Adam that he is the creature, for only the Creator knows what is good and what is evil for the creatures. What is death and what is evil, Adam knows not. But through the prohibition of the tree Adam knows that God is saying, "Adam, thou art as thou art because of me, thy Creator; so be as thou art. Thou art a free creature, so be a creature."[17] God tempts no one. Since Adam does not know what death is, this prohibition is no longer a threat, but God's grace. Hence, in speaking of Adam, Bonhoeffer writes:

> He understands the prohibition and the threat of death only as a fresh gift, the grace of God. The limit is grace because it is the basis of creatureliness and freedom; the limit is the middle. Grace is that which supports man over the abyss of non-being, non-living, that which is not created-and all this nothingness is only conceivable to Adam in the form of the giving grace of God.[18]

Bonhoeffer *and* Wu Wei

There are striking similarities between Bonhoeffer's and the Taoist approach to spirituality. Both provide similar critiques to the attempt of human beings in dealing with the problem of the anxiety of the soul. Bonhoeffer suggests that one cannot try to overcome this guilt or the inauthenticity of being through the knowledge of good and evil, because the knowledge of good and evil presupposes the disunity between being and Being. Taoism teaches that the way to the Way is not through splitting between right and wrong, good and bad.

The authentic person is one who is rid of this dichotomy through the process of reduction. There is no "ought-to-be" because the "is" is already good enough. Similarly, spontaneity takes place when one learns to overcome this knowledge of good and evil.

In speaking of the commandment, Bonhoeffer affirms that this commandment becomes the command to live because through grace one is free to act. "It allows the flood of life to flow freely. It lets man eat, drink, sleep, work, rest and play. It does not interrupt man." This is also clearly reflected in the concept *wu wei*. *Wu wei* is acting that takes place spontaneously. It is spontaneous because it is free. It is free from the dichotomy between good and bad, knowledge and ignorance, words and silence. One does not need to try to be anything but oneself. One can act freely because this being is no longer being dictated through cognitive construction.

Bonhoeffer also suggests that the tree of the knowledge of good and evil is the tree of life in that it promises that if Adam were to respect this limit, life will be given to him. This concept is also prominent in Taoist philosophy. One needs to learn to recognize the importance of nonbeing. One needs to learn to recognize that one is finite. Happiness and sadness, pleasure and pain, life and death, these are facts in life. In this finiteness one must realize that the Infinite, the Way, cannot be grasped. It is beyond our category of thinking.

Pastoral Theology

How can we relate this concept to pastoral theology? Pastoral theology refers to the theology that informs the practice of pastoral ministry. This theology must be rooted in our understanding of God and reality. To believe in God is to believe that we are creatures. We are finite beings who inherit, within our ontological structure, that connection with that which transcends. Hence belief in God presupposes finitude as its necessary ontological structure. What is the theological implication of this presupposition to the practice of pastoral ministry?

Theology is a study of God. To study is to come to an understanding of the object of our study. Finitude, on the other hand, is the recognition of our limitations. Finitude speaks to the recognition of our limitations and the awareness of the infinite. Hence the theology that presupposes finitude is the theology that recognizes, first and foremost, human limitations in the understanding of God, the Infinite. God that can be known is not the eternal God. This reminds us of the first chapter of *Tao Te Ching* when Lao Tzu states, "The tao that can be told is not the eternal *Tao*. The name that can be named is not the eternal Name."[19] This name is incomprehensible. When Tozan (807-869) was asked the question, "What is Zen?" He replied, "Three pounds of flax!"[20] This eccentric answer aims at cutting off intellectual reasoning implied in the question. The question does not exist. According to Panikkar, silence is the answer to the question regarding absolute reality. The answer is to silence the question itself and in this silence we are invited to "total acceptance of our human condition, of the real contingency in which we find ourselves" because to "thirst is to transgress Reality, to evade the human situation."[21] The real contingency of ourselves needs to be embraced.

Pastoral theology that is based on the concept of finitude is the theology that accepts the mystery of God and embraces nonbeing as an essential part of human ontological structure. Finitude is central to Christian theology. It speaks of human limitations. It speaks of the fall. It acknowledges Being as the very ground of human beings. It speaks of courage to face reality. It removes God from the boundary of human limitations and places God as a source of strength. On the other hand, if we ignore nonbeing as a qualitative aspect of human beings we are actually moving toward the divinization of the self.

On the basis of finitude, the acceptance of the mystery of God and the recognition of nonbeing form the basis of our ministry. By so doing, we are called to participate fully in the reality as it presents itself to us. What does it mean to participate fully in this reality? Bonhoeffer reflects:

> [It is o]nly by living completely in this world that one learns to have faith. One must completely abandon any attempt to make something of oneself, whether it be a saint, or a converted sinner, or a churchman (a so-called priestly type!), a righteous man or an unrighteous one, a sick man or a healthy one. By this worldliness I mean living unreservedly in life's duties, problems, success and failures, experiences and perplexities. In so doing we throw ourselves completely into the arms of God, tak-

ing seriously, not our own sufferings, but those of God in the world, watching with Christ in Gethsemane.[22]

Our ministry must be rooted in the joy and hope, pain and despair of people to whom we are ministering. We are asked to enter their reality, to sit with them within this reality. In entering this reality we are called to the recognition of the God who works in mysterious ways and hence to remain open and allow God to speak to us. This is faith. This is the faith we need to invite our congregation to engage in. Speaking of this invitation Moore writes, "We have to arrive at that difficult point where we don't know what is going on or what we can do. That precise point is an opening to true faith."[23]

QUESTIONS ON MORAL IMPLICATIONS

One of the questions I hear when I explain this principle to my colleagues is "If we are to move beyond defining the 'ought' will this not be a way of escaping our moral obligations?" I would like to briefly state that a person who practices *wu wei* is not amoral. *Wu wei* may appear to be antinomous because it does not concern itself with what is normative. If we look carefully, it is not that *wu wei* does not address the question of what is normative but rather, it questions the basic assumptions of norms and offers an individual the freedom "to be" within the reality of nonbeing itself. Hence Chuang Tzu's advice to empty the "ought" may be viewed as an invitation to reframe our understanding of reality. In this understanding of reality, one is invited to align oneself with the flow of life instead of trying to cognitively capture and manipulate reality. If ethics emerge from one's values and one's values are derived from one's understanding of reality, then what Lao Tzu and Chuang Tzu proposed may also be defined as moral and ethical since *wu wei* invites us to reevaluate our understanding of reality upon which we based our moral principles.

The moral implications of *wu wei* require much greater space than we can address in this book. For the purposes of this book it may be said that the practice of the principle of *wu wei* within the context of depressed individuals seeks mainly to empty the constructs of the "ought to be" which, in most cases, occur because of the inordinate unrealistic guilt and the negativity that escalates the depressive cycle. Within this context, *wu wei* is not about disregarding morality but deconstructing unrealistic expectations through the process of emptying so that one may see more clearly.

SUMMARY:
WU WEI, *DEPRESSION,*
AND PASTORAL CARE

Lao Tzu and Chuang Tzu teach that the *Tao* cannot be comprehended, analyzed, and captured by rationality. But too often we are driven by the urge for security to try to grasp the *Tao*. We are driven by the anxiety of being to try to find a solid ground upon which we can stand and feel safe. We experience what philosopher Richard Bernstein calls "the Cartesian anxiety":

> Descartes' search for a foundation or Archimedean point is more than a device to solve metaphysical and epistemological problems. It is the quest for some fixed point, some stable rock upon which we can secure our lives against the vicissitudes that constantly threaten us. . . . Either there is some support for our being, a fixed foundation for our knowledge, or we cannot escape the forces of darkness that envelop us with madness, with intellectual and moral chaos.[24]

We search for this epistemological basis in an attempt to rest our souls. In an attempt to cope with the anxiety of nonbeing, we move farther away from the *Tao,* the Way. We think we need to grasp and struggle in order to reach the *Tao*. But we, in turn, become further removed from the *Tao* because we do not realize that we are already there. The *Tao* just is. We do not need to go anywhere else. We need to learn to stay right here.

Similarly, depressed people need to learn to stay right here. In the pain of negativity, depressed individuals journey away from themselves by struggling and trying to overcome this negativity, but what is needed is for them to sit in this experience. The struggle only further entangles. The struggle leads them away from themselves. A depleted self can only destroy itself. But the self that embraces nonbeing discovers, in the face of negativity, the possibility of being. It discovers that "all spiritual traditions undercut our attachments and allegiances that we lean on for security, for these are the very things that lead us to defend, impose, and attack."[25] This journey is the journey back to the self as is.

This is why *wu wei* is not only the way to the Tao but the way depressed individuals can journey back to themselves. Only the self that has finally returned home to itself, that has befriended nonbeing and its shadow, can rediscover meaning and worth. This is why this principle of *wu wei* has significant theological implications for pastoral caregivers in helping depressed people. Our care becomes pastoral when it speaks of meaning. When it discovers meaning even in the face of nonbeing, care moves from counseling and therapy to spirituality. Such care speaks to the soul.

Notes

Introduction

1. Ian H. Gotlib and Constance L. Hammen, *Psychological Aspects of Depression: Toward a Cognitive-Interpersonal Integration* (New York: John Wiley and Sons, 1992), iv, 1.

2. Martin E. P. Seligman, "Why Is There So Much Depression Today? The Waxing of the Individual and the Waning of the Commons," in *Contemporary Psychological Approaches to Depression: Theory, Research, and Treatment,* ed. Rick E. Ingram (New York: Plenum Press, 1990), 5.

3. Seligman, "Why Is There So Much Depression Today?", 8.

4. Howard Stone, *Depression and Hope: New Insights for Pastoral Counseling* (Minneapolis: Fortress Press, 1998), xi.

5. Gayle Belsher and Charles G. Costello, "Relapse After Recovery from Unipolar Depression: A Critical Review," *Psychological Bulletin* 104, no. 1 (1988): 84-96; see also Gerald L. Klerman and Myrna M. Weissman, "Course, Morbidity, and Costs of Depression," *Archives of General Psychiatry* 49 (1992): 831-834.

6. Gotlib and Hammen, *Psychological Aspects of Depression,* 1.

7. David Karp, *Speaking of Sadness: Depression, Disconnection, and the Meanings of Illness* (New York: Oxford University Press, 1996), 10.

8. Leslie A. Robinson, Jeffrey S. Berman, and Robert A. Neimeyer, "Psychotherapy for the Treatment of Depression: A Comprehensive Review of Controlled Outcome Research," *Psychological Bulletin* 108, no. 1 (1990): 40.

9. Karp, *Speaking of Sadness,* 24.

10. Ibid., 47.

11. Aaron T. Beck, *Depression: Causes and Treatments* (Philadelphia: University of Pennsylvania Press, 1972), 17-23.

12. These standards may be defined in relational terms such as, "I should have been more generous" or "I should not have been so blunt."

13. Tom Pyszczynski and Jeff Greenberg, *Hanging On and Letting Go: Understanding the Onset, Progression, and Remission of Depression* (New York: Springer-Verlag, 1992), 49.

14. Pyszczynski and Greenberg, *Hanging On and Letting Go,* 9.

15. Ibid., 107.

16. Ibid., 114.

17. Lao Tzu, *Tao Te Ching: A New English Version,* trans. Stephen Mitchell (New York: Harper and Row, 1988), 41.

Chapter 1

1. David Karp, *Speaking of Sadness: Depression, Disconnection, and the Meaning of Illness* (New York: Oxford University Press, 1996), 22.

2. Richard Dayringer, *Dealing with Depression: Five Pastoral Interventions* (Binghamton, New York: The Haworth Pastoral Press, 1995), 2-3. Gilbert identifies three marks of clinical depression: (1) hereditary predisposition; (2) childhood background that relates to emotional deprivation; and (3) existential situations that provoke stress to the level where coping becomes almost impossible. Binford Gilbert, *The Pastoral Care of Depression: A Guidebook* (Binghamton, NY: The Haworth Press), 17.

3. Ian H. Gotlib and Constance L. Hammen, *Psychological Aspects of Depression: Toward a Cognitive-Interpersonal Integration* (New York: John Wiley and Sons, 1992), 2.

4. Karp, *Speaking of Sadness*, 57.

5. American Psychiatric Association, *Diagnostic and Statistical Manual of Mental Disorders* (DSM-IV), Fourth Edition, (Washington DC: American Psychiatric Association, 1994), 327.

6. Harold I. Kaplan, Benjamin J. Sadock, and Jack A. Grebb, *Kaplan and Sadock's Synopsis of Psychiatry: Behavioral Sciences, Clinical Psychiatry,* Seventh Edition (Baltimore: Williams and Wilkins, 1994), 531.

7. Karp, *Speaking of Sadness*, 41.

8. Lee N. Robins, John E. Helzer, Myrna Weissman, Helen Orvaschel, Ernest Greenberg, Jack D. Burke, Jr., and Darrel A. Regier, "Lifetime Prevalence of Specific Psychiatric Disorders in Three Sites," *Archives of General Psychiatry* 41, no. 10 (1984): 949-958.

9. This study is a part of the National Institute of Mental Health Clinical Research Branch Collaborative Program on the Psychobiology of Depressive Clinical Study.

10. ECA is a corroborative effort to apply common diagnostic and health instruments to large general population samples.

11. Gerald Klerman, Philip W. Lavori, John Rice, Theodore Reich, Jean Endicott, Nancy C. Andreasen, Martin B. Keller, and Robert M. A. Hirschfield, "Birth Cohort Trends in Rates of Major Depressive Disorder Among Relatives of Patients with Affective Disorder" *Archives of General Psychiatry* 42 (1985): 689-693.

12. Myrna Weissman and J. Myers, "Affective Disorders in a United States Urban Community: The Use of Research Diagnostic Criteria in an Epidemiological Survey," *Archives of General Psychiatry* 38 (1978): 1304-1311.

13. Jeffrey Boyd and Myrna Weissman, "Epidemiology of Affective Disorders," *Archives of General Psychiatry* 38 (1981): 1039-1046.

14. Gotlib and Hammen, *Psychological Aspects of Depression*, ix.

15. Dayringer, *Dealing with Depression*, 1. Gotlib and Hammen's estimation is between 9 to 20 percent of the US population. *Psychological Aspects of Depression*, 1.

16. Ian H. Gotlib and Catherine A. Colby, *Treatment of Depression: An Interpersonal Systems Approach* (New York: Pergamon Press, 1987), ix.

17. Dayringer, *Dealing with Depression*, 2.

18. Gotlib and Colby, *Treatment of Depression*, ix.

19. Paula J. Clayton, "Prevalence and Course of Affective Disorders," in *Depression: Basic Mechanisms, Diagnosis, and Treatment*, eds. A. John Rush and Kenneth Z. Altshuler (New York: Guilford Press, 1986), 33.

20. John Wing and Paul Bebbington, "Epidemiology of Depression," in *Handbook of Depression: Treatment, Assessment and Research*, eds. Ernest Edward Beckham and William Leber (Homewood, IL: Dorsey Press, 1985), 771.

21. See, for example, Susan Dunlap, *Counseling Depressed Women* (Louisville: Westminster John Knox Press, 1997), 40.

22. Christie C. Neuger, "Women's Depression: Lives at Risk," in *Women in Travail and Transition: A New Pastoral Care*, eds. Maxine Glaz and Jeanne Stevenson Moessner (Minneapolis: Fortress Press, 1991), 150.

23. Nolen-Hoeksema, *Sex Differences in Depression* (Stanford: Stanford University Press, 1990). See also Howard Stone, *Depression and Hope: New Insights for Pastoral Counseling* (Minneapolis: Fortress Press, 1990), 42-44.

24. Susan Nolen-Hoeksema, Joan S. Girgus, and Martin E. P. Seligman, "Sex Differences in Depression and Explanatory Style in Children," *Journal of Youth and Adolescence* 20, no. 2 (1991), 234-235.

25. Peter M. Lewinsohn, Edward M. Duncan, Alyn K. Stanton, and Martin Hautzinger, "Age at First Onset for Nonbipolar Depression," *Journal of Abnormal Psychology* 95 (1986), 378-383.

26. Gotlib and Hammen, *Psychological Aspects of Depression*, 25.

27. Kaplan, Sadock, and Grebb, *Kaplan and Sadock's Synopsis of Psychiatry*, 517.

28. Mryna Weissman and Cross-National Collaborative Group, "The Changing Rate of Major Depression," *Journal of the American Medical Association* 268, no. 21 (1992): 3098-3104. For cross-cultural studies on depression, see Wing and Bebbington, "Epidemiology of Depression," 765-794.

29. Harold Koenig, "Religion and Health in Later life," in *Aging, Spirituality and Religion*, eds. M. A. Kimble, S. H. McFadden, J. W. Ellor, and J. J. Seeber (Minneapolis: Fortress, 1995), 9-29. See also Dan G. Blazer, *Depression in Late Life* (St. Louise, MA: Mosby, 1993), 7-22.

30. Martin E. P. Seligman, "Why Is There So Much Depression Today? The Waxing of the Individual and the Waning of the Commons," in *Contemporary Psychological Approaches to Depression: Theory, Research, and Treatment*, ed. Rick E. Ingram (New York: Plenum Press, 1990), 1-9.

31. Lewinsohn, Duncan, Stanton, and Hautzinger, "Age at First Onset for Nonbipolar Depression," 380.

32. Martin B. Keller, Robert W. Shapiro, Philip W. Lavori, and Nicola Wolfe, "Relapse in Major Depressive Disorder," *Archives of General Psychiatry* 39 (1982): 911-915. Predictors for increased risk were identified. These are (a) the presence of chronic depression within two years and (b) a history of three previous courses of affective episodes. It is important to note too that Keller and Shapiro did not provide criteria that will exclude patients with a history of mania, hypomania, and minor depressive disorder. Gayle Belsher and Charles G. Costello, "Relapse After Recovery

from Unipolar Depression: A Critical Review," *Psychological Bulletin* 104, no. 1 (1988): 87.

33. Martin B. Keller, Philip W. Lavori, Jean Endicott, William Coryell, and Gerald L. Klerman, "Double Depression: Two-Year Follow-Up," *American Journal of Psychiatry* 44 (1983): 692.

34. National Institute of Mental Health/National Institute of Health (NIMH/NIH) Consensus Development Conference Statement, "Mood Disorders: Pharmacologic Prevention of Recurrences," *American Journal of Psychiatry* 142 (1985): 471.

35. Belsher and Costello, "Relapse After Recovery from Unipolar Depression," 84-96. Both Belsher and Costello, in reviewing studies of relapse, are aware of the inadequate definitions of recovery and relapse, the difficulty in selecting the samples, and the need for greater precision in what is to be included or excluded in setting the criteria to determine relapse.

36. According to Kaplan and Sadock, an untreated depressive episode lasts six to thirteen months while most treated episodes last about three months. As the course of depression progresses, patients tend to have more frequent episodes that last longer. The mean number of episodes over the course of twenty years is between five to six. Kaplan, Sadock, and Grebb, *Kaplan and Sadock's Synopsis of Psychiatry,* 538-539.

37. Clayton, "Prevalence and Course of Affective Disorders," 34-35.

38. Gotlib and Hammen, *Psychological Aspects of Depression,* 29-31.

39. Kaplan, Sadock, and Grebb, *Kaplan and Sadock's Synopsis of Psychiatry,* 517.

40. A. John Rush, "Diagnosis of Affective Disorder," in *Depression: Basic Mechanisms, Diagnosis, and Treatment,* eds. A. John Rush and Kenneth Z. Altshuler (New York: Guilford Press, 1986), 2.

41. Kaplan, Sadock, and Grebb, *Kaplan and Sadock's Synopsis of Psychiatry,* 517.

42. Sigmund Freud, *The Freud Reader,* ed. Peter Gay (New York: W. W. Norton, 1989), 587.

43. Rush, "Diagnosis of Affective Disorder," 2-4.

Chapter 2

1. David Karp, *Speaking of Sadness: Depression, Disconnection, and the Meaning of Illness* (New York: Oxford University Press, 1996), 63.

2. Harold I. Kaplan, Benjamin J. Sadock, and Jack A. Grebb, *Kaplan and Sadock's Synopsis of Psychiatry: Behavioral Sciences, Clinical Psychiatry,* Seventh Edition (Baltimore: Williams and Wilkins, 1994), 522.

3. Kaplan, Sadock, and Grebb, *Kaplan and Sadock's Synopsis of Psychiatry,* 523. This is the process of sensitization where an initial stimulus may cause little response. The repetition of this stimulus may lead to a full response. The continuation of this exposure results in lesser and lesser levels of stimulus in order to trigger full response. Over time the response occurs spontaneously even in the absence of any stimulus. Robert J. Hedaya, *Understanding Biological Psychiatry* (New York: W. W. Norton, 1996), 66-67.

4. Paula J. Clayton, "Prevalence and Course of Affective Disorders," in *Depression: Basic Mechanisms, Diagnosis, and Treatment,* eds. A. John Rush and Kenneth Z. Altshuler (New York: Guilford Press, 1986), 32-44.

5. Andrew Billings and Rudolf Moos, "Psychosocial Stressors, Coping, and Depression," in *Handbook of Depression: Treatment, Assessment, and Research,* eds. Ernest Beckham and William Leber (Homewood, IL: Dorsey Press, 1985), 944.

6. Billings and Moos, "Psychosocial Stressors, Coping, and Depression," 950.

7. Clayton, "Prevalence and Course of Affective Disorders," 35.

8. Kaplan, Sadock, and Grebb, *Kaplan and Sadock's Synopsis of Psychiatry,* 523.

9. Ian H. Gotlib and Catherine A. Colby, *Treatment of Depression: An Interpersonal Systems Approach* (New York, Pergamon Press, 1987), 11-12.

10. Tirril Harris, George W. Brown, and A. Bifulco, "Loss of Parent in Childhood and Adult Psychiatric Disorder: The Role of Lack of Adequate Parental Care," *Psychological Medicine* 16 (1986): 641-659.

11. This study was based on 714 depressed adult inpatients and 387 nondepressed, nonpatient individuals. Thomas Crook, Allen Raskin, and John Eliot, "Parent-child Relationships and Adult Depression," *Child Development* 52 (1981): 950-957.

12. Gotlib and Colby, *Treatment of Depression,* 10.

13. George W. Brown and Tirril Harris, *Social Origins of Depression: A Study of Psychiatric Disorder in Women* (New York: Free Press, 1978, p. A9).

14. S. Henderson, D. G. Byrne, and P. Duncan-Jones. *Neurosis and the Social Environment* (New York: Academic Press, 1981).

15. Myrna M. Weissman, "Advances in Psychiatric Epidemiology: Rates and Risks for Depression," *American Journal of Public Health* 77 (1987): 445-451.

16. Frederic W. Ilfeld, "Current Social Stressors and Symptoms of Depression," *American Journal of Psychiatry* 134 (1977): 161-166.

17. Lars Freden, *Psychosocial Aspects of Depression: No Way Out?* (Chichester, NY: John Wiley and Sons, 1982).

18. Susan Dunlap, *Counseling Depressed Women* (Louisville: Westminister John Knox Press, 1997), 36.

19. Barbara Dohrenwend, Patrick E. Shrout, B. Link, J. Martin, and Andrew Skodol, "Overview and Initial Results from a Risk-factor Study of Depression and Schizophrenia," in *Mental Disorders in the Community: Progress and Challenges,* ed. James Elmer Barrett (New York: Guilford Press, 1986).

20. Richard S. Lazarus and Susan Folkman, *Stress, Appraisal, and Coping* (New York: Springer Verlag, 1984).

21. Brown and Harris, *Social Origins of Depression,* 19.

22. Charles J. Holahan and Rudolf H. Moos, "Life Stressors, Personal and Social Resources, and Depression: A Four-Year Structural Model," *Journal of Abnormal Psychology* 100 (1991): 31-38; Peter M. Lewinhson, Harry M. Hoberman, and M. Rosenbaum, "A Prospective Study of Risk Factors for Unipolar Depression," *Journal of Abnormal Psychology* 97 (1988): 251-264.

23. Ian H. Gotlib and Constance L. Hammen, *Psychological Aspects of Depression: Toward a Cognitive-Interpersonal Integration* (New York: John Wiley and Sons, 1992), 148.

24. Dunlap, *Counseling Depressed Women*, 7.

25. Gotlib and Hammen, *Psychological Aspects of Depression*, 149.

26. Gerald J. Tortora, *Principles of Human Anatomy* (New York: HarperCollins Publishers, 1992), 464.

27. Sid Gilman and Sarah W. Newman, *Manter and Gatz's Essentials of Clinical Neuroanatomy and Neurophysiology*, Eighth Edition (Philadelphia: F.A. Davis, 1992), 25.

28. Tortora, *Principles of Human Anatomy*, 465.

29. Kaplan, Sadock, and Grebb, *Kaplan and Sadock's Synopsis of Psychiatry*, 518.

30. James H. Scully, *Psychiatry* (Media, PA: Harwal Publishing, 1985), 55.

31. Edmund J. Bourne, *The Anxiety and Phobia Workbook* (Oakland, CA: New Harbinger Publications, 1990), 30.

32. Christopher Peterson, Steven F. Maier, and Martin E. P. Seligman, *Learned Helplessness: A Theory for the Age of Personal Control* (Oxford: Oxford University Press, 1993), 62.

33. Kaplan, Sadock, and Grebb, *Kaplan and Sadock's Synopsis of Psychiatry*, 139. The epinephrine system and the norepinephrine system are also referred to as, respectively, the adrenergic system and the noradrenergic system.

34. Ibid., 576.

35. Ibid., 518-519

36. Ibid., 519.

37. Peterson, Maier, and Seligman, 67.

38. T. C. Neylan, "Treatment of Sleep Disturbances in Depressed Patients," *Journal of Clinical Psychiatry* 56, no. 2 (1995): 56-61.

39. Hedaya, *Understanding Biological Psychiatry*, 110.

40. Ibid., 111.

41. Ibid., 110-111.

42. Monte S. Buchsbaum, H. H. Holcomb, L. DeLisi, and E. Hazlett, "Brain Imaging in Affective Disorders," in *Depression: Basic Mechanisms, Diagnosis, and Treatment*, eds. A. John Rush and Kenneth Z. Altshuler (New York: Guilford Press, 1986), 129.

43. Ibid., 129-130.

44. Hedaya, *Understanding Biological Psychiatry*, 116. See also Buchsbaum, Holcomb, DeLisi, and Hazlett, *"Brain Imaging in Affective Disorders,"* 137-138.

45. Hedaya, *Understanding Biological Psychiatry*, 161-166; Richard Dayringer, *Dealing with Depression: Five Pastoral Interventions* (Binghamton, New York: The Haworth Pastoral Press, 1995), 109. Shelly F. Greenfield, Roger D. Weiss, Larry R. Muenz, Lisa M. Vagge, John F. Kelly, Lisa R. Bello, and Jacqueline Michael, "The Effect of Depression on Return to Drinking: A Prospective Study," *Archive of General Psychiatry* 55, no. 3 (1998): 259-265.

46. Michael A. Schlesser "Neuroendocrine Abnormalities in Affective Disorders," in *Depression: Basic Mechanisms, Diagnosis, and Treatment*, eds. A. John

Rush and Kenneth Z. Altshuler (New York: Guilford Press, 1986), 49; David J. Janowsky and S. Craig Risch, "Adrenergic-Cholinergic Balance and Affective Disorders," in *Depression: Basic Mechanism, Diagnosis, and Treatment*, eds. A. John Rush and Kenneth Z. Altshuler (New York: Guilford Press, 1986), 84-85.

47. M. L. Odens and C. H. Fox, "Adult Sleep Apnea Syndromes," *American Family Physician* 52, no. 3 (1995): 856-866.

48. Patients with pancreatic cancer exhibit the symptoms of severe depression. This is rather common among men between fifty and seventy years of age. It is also accompanied by abdominal pain that radiates to the back and weight loss. These patients, although exhibiting symptoms of depression, do not experience guilt neither do they have previous psychiatric history.

49. Hedaya, *Understanding Biological Psychiatry*, 241. The exceptions to this rule are hormones (such as thyroid, estrogen, progesterone that have to do with cell nucleus) and lithium (whose site may be at the level of the cell membrane or one of the internal proteins).

50. Ibid., 242.

51. Katherine M. Noll, John M. Davis, and Frank DeLeon-Jones, "Medication and Somatic Therapies in the Treatment of Depression," in *Handbook of Depression: Treatment, Assessment, and Research*, eds. Ernest E. Beckham and William R. Leber (Homewood, IL: Dorsey Press, 1985), 237-238.

52. Hedaya, *Understanding Biological Psychiatry*, 258-259.

53. Kaplan, Sadock, and Grebb, *Kaplan and Sadock's Synopsis of Psychiatry*, 545. The improvement related to poor sleep and appetite is more true with tricyclic drugs than with SSRIs.

54. Ibid., 551.

55. Dayringer, *Dealing with Depression*, 113.

56. Noll, Davis, and DeLeon-Jones, "Medication and Somatic Therapies in the Treatment of Depression," 274.

57. Kaplan, Sadock, and Grebb, *Kaplan and Sadock's Synopsis of Psychiatry*, 1005-1006.

Chapter 3

1. Howard Stone, *Depression and Hope: New Insights for Pastoral Counseling* (Minneapolis: Fortress Press, 1990), 21.

2. Brooks E. Holifield, *A History of Pastoral Care in America: From Salvation to Self-Realization* (Nashville: Abingdon Press, 1983), 15-31.

3. Stone, *Depression and Hope*, 22. See also Roy W. Fairchild, "Sadness and Depression," in *Dictionary of Pastoral Care and Counseling*, ed. Rodney J. Hunter (Nashville: Abingdon Press, 1990), 1103-1106.

4. Martin Luther, *Luther's Works*, vol. 33, eds. Philip S. Watson and Helmut T. Lehmann (Philadelphia: Fortress Press, 1972), 190.

5. Stone, *Depression and Hope*, 27-28.

6. Holifield, *A History of Pastoral Care in America*, 111.

7. Listen O. Mills, "Pastoral Care: History, Tradition, and Definitions," in *Dictionary of Pastoral Care and Counseling,* 1990, ed. Rodney J. Hunter (Nashville: Abingdon Press, 1990), 842.

8. Holifield, *A History of Pastoral Care in America,* 36-37; Mills "Pastoral Care," 836-844.

9. Cabot was a leading neurologist, cardiologist, and professor of medicine at Harvard, who became the founder of medical social work and of clinical pathological conferences for medical teaching. He believed that clinical training would help to provide character development. Boisen was a graduate of Union Theological Seminary (New York).

10. Holifield, *A History of Pastoral Care in America,* 245.

11. Howard Stone, "Depression," in *Handbook for Basic Types of Pastoral Care and Counseling,* eds. Howard Stone and William M. Clements (Nashville: Abingdon Press, 1991), 179-208.

12. Ibid., 182-183.

13. The four most widely used assessment tools for depression are Beck's Depression Inventory (BDI), the Minnesota Multiphasic Personality Inventory (MMPI-D) (depression) Scale, Zung Self-Rating Depression Scale (SDS), and The Hamilton Rating Scale for Depression (HRSD). For further information see David J. Berndt, "Inventories and Scales," in *Depressive Disorders: Facts, Theories, and Treatment Methods,* eds. Benjamin B. Wolman and George Stricker (New York: John Wiley and Sons, 1990), 255-274.

14. By affective treatment Stone refers to the showing of care, warmth, and empathy and allowing depressed individuals to express themselves.

15. Physiological intervention here refers to the use of medication. Stone emphasizes the importance for ministers to have some knowledge of medication used by depressed individuals in their treatment and the side effects. For example, it is important for depressed individuals to understand that it takes at least ten to fourteen days for medication to take effect.

16. Stone, *Depression and Hope,* 54.

17. Ibid., 120-122. See also Stone, "Depression," 179-208.

18. Fairchild, "Sadness and Depression," 1103-1106.

19. Richard Dayringer and Myron C. Madden, "Pastoral Counseling Dealing with Depression," in *Dealing with Depression: Five Pastoral Interventions,* ed. Richard Dayringer (Binghamton, NY: The Haworth Press, 1995), 37.

20. Binford Gilbert, *The Pastoral Care of Depression: A Guidebook* (Binghamton, NY: The Haworth Press), 73.

21. Ibid., 65-74.

22. Rebecca L. Propst, *Psychotherapy in a Religious Framework: Spirituality in the Emotional Healing Process* (New York: Human Sciences Press, 1988, 121-141).

23. Susan Dunlap, *Counseling Depressed Women* (Louisville: Westminister John Knox Press, 1997), 112.

24. John J. O'Hearne and Richard Dayringer, "Transactional Analysis Dealing with Depression," in *Dealing with Depression: Five Pastoral Interventions,* ed. Richard Dayringer (Binghamton, NY: The Haworth Press, 1995), 23; see also Fairchild, "Sadness and Depression," 1103-1106.

25. Dunlap, *Counseling Depressed Women,* 40.

26. Ibid., 46-47.

27. Christie C. Neuger, "Women's Depression: Lives at Risk," in *Women in Travail and Transition: A New Pastoral Care,* eds. Maxine Glaz and Jeanne Stevenson Moessner (Minneapolis: Fortress Press, 1991), 146-161.

28. Ibid., 151.

29. Nolen-Hoeksema's studies of gender differences in depression show that women's risk of depression, which is higher than men, can be accounted for by their styles of coping. While men tend to distract, women ruminate. It is this act of rumination that leads to deterioration in depressive symptoms. Susan Nolen-Hoeksema, *Sex Differences in Depression* (Stanford: Stanford University Press, 1990). Similarities of this approach in comparison to that of self-regulatory perseveration are affirmed in a letter which professor Pyszczynski wrote to me as a reply to my inquiry regarding recent research on this theory. In the letter he states, "The 'Hanging on and letting go' book is the most recent review of that literature. Nolen-Hoeksema's work on rumination is very closely related to our work though, and she has done quite a bit of research since that time." Tom Pyszczynski, letter to author, August 27, 1998.

30. Mary Louise Bringle, " 'I Just Can't Stop Thinking About It': Depression Rumination, and Forgiveness," *Word and World* 16, no. 3 (1996): 340-346.

31. Mary Louise Bringle, "Soul-Dye and Salt: Integrating Spiritual and Medical Understandings of Depression," *Journal of Pastoral Care* 50, no. 4 (1996), 338. In *Despairing: Sickness or Sin?,* Bringle discusses the importance of balance. There is the need to see light in despair because the person who dares to despair, dares to hope as well. But, as Christians, we must not allow despair to triumph. While despair may continue to remain with us, we need to celebrate Christ who is among us as well. Mary Louise Bringle, *Despair: Sickness or Sin? Hopelessness and Healing in the Christian Life* (Nashville: Abingdon Press, 1990).

32. Bringle, "Soul-Dye and Salt," 339.

Chapter 4

1. Lao-Tzu, *Tao Te Ching: A New English Version,* trans. Stephen Mitchell (New York: Harper and Row, 1988), 9.

2. David Rosen, *Transforming Depression* (New York: Penguin Books, 1993), 14.

3. Ian H. Gotlib and Constance L. Hammen, *Psychological Aspects of Depression: Toward a Cognitive-Interpersonal Integration* (New York: John Wiley and Sons, 1992), 149.

4. Tom Pyszczynski and Jeff Greenberg, *Hanging On and Letting Go: Understanding the Onset, Progression, and Remission of Depression* (New York: Springer-Verlag, 1992), 9.

5. Ibid., 8-9.

6. Ibid., 49.

7. Gotlib and Hammen, *Psychological Aspects of Depression,* 260-262.

8. David A. Karp, *Speaking of Sadness: Depression, Disconnection, and the Meaning of Illness* (New York: Oxford University Press, 1996), 29. This quotation is based on an interview by David Karp with one of his subjects who suffers clinical depression.

9. Ibid., 28.

10. William Styron, *Darkness Visible: A Memoir of Madness* (New York: Vintage Books, 1990), 46.

11. Susan J. Dunlap, *Counseling Depressed Women* (Louisville: Westminster John Knox Press, 1997), 1.

12. Thomas Moore, *Care of Soul: A Guide for Cultivating Depth and Sacredness in Everyday Life* (New York: HarperPerennial, 1992), 138.

13. Cognitive therapy believes that negative thoughts make one vulnerable to depression since mood is the result of one's belief. Many social psychologists tend to disagree with this position. Hammen suggests that negative cognition is not the effect of thinking on depression but the effect of depression on thinking. This is so, argues Hammen, because when people are depressed they display negative thinking but when not depressed they do not exhibit negative thoughts. Constance Hammen, "Vulnerability to Depression: Personal, Situational, and Family Aspects," *Contemporary Psychological Approaches to Depression: Theory, Research, and Treatment*, ed. Rick E. Ingram (New York: Plenum Press, 1990), 60. Keith S. Dobson and Brian F. Shaw's research suggests that depressed patients who improved after treatment do not exhibit bias recall of negative words. Keith S. Dobson and Brian F. Shaw, "Specificity and Stability of Self-Referent Encoding in Clinical Depression," *Journal of Abnormal Psychology* 96 (1987): 34-40; see also Gotlib and Hammen, *Psychological Aspects of Depression,* 137. However there is a strong suggestion, too, that some form of cognitive vulnerability may exist prior to the course of depression. In discussing the cognitive-interpersonal approach to the understanding of depression, Gotlib and Hammen believe that early experiences of a person predispose one toward depression later in life. Gotlib and Hammen, *Psychological Aspects of Depression,* 248. Even though there is no conclusive evidence to prove that negative cognition causes depression, it is reasonable to state that some form of negative pattern of thinking exists that may result in clinical depression.

14. Aaron T. Beck, *Depression: Causes and Treatments* (Philadelphia: University of Pennsylvania Press, 1972), 255. J. Mark G. Williams, *The Psychological Treatment of Depression: A Guide to the Theory and Practice of Cognitive-Behavior Therapy* (New York: Free Press, 1984), 16-17; Gotlib and Hammen, *Psychological Aspects of Depression,* 114.

15. Gotlib and Hammen, *Psychological Aspects of Depressison,* 114.

16. Alexander M. Buchwald. "Depressive Mood and Estimates of Reinforcement Frequency," *Journal of Abnormal Psychology* 86 (1977): 443-46; Ian H. Gotlib, "Self-reinforcement and Recall: Differential Deficits in Depressed and Nondepressed Psychiatric Patients," *Journal of Abnormal Psychology* 90 (1981), 521-530; Ian H. Gotlib, "Perception and Recall of Interpersonal Feedback: Negative Bias in Depression," *Cognitive Therapy and Research* 7 (1983), 399-412.

17. Lora Lee Sloan, "Processing Strategies and Recall Performance for Narrative Passages and Word Lists of Negative and Neutral Affective Valence in Depression

(Memory Deficits)" (PhD diss., University of North Dakota, 1997). There are researchers who fail to find significant differences among depressed and nondepressed individuals. Explanation for this lack of significant differences includes the need to consider the severity of depression, the interaction of the type of schema and the nature of the feedback, interpersonal skills of the subjects, and the possibility that it is the nondepressed individuals who distort the environment in the positive direction while the depressed are more realistic. Gotlib and Hammen, *Psychological Aspects of Depression*, 114-117. For explanation on the last point see also Lauren B. Alloy, Jeanne S. Albright, Lyn Y. Abramson, and Benjamin M. Dykman, "Depressive Realism and Nondeprssive Optimistic Illusions: The Role of the Self," in *Contemporary Psychological Approaches to Depression: Theory, Research, and Treatment*, ed. Rick E. Ingram (New York: Plenum Press, 1990), 71-86.

18. Gotlib and Hammen, *Psychological Aspects of Depression*, 129.

19. Ibid., 115.

20. Alfred S. Friedman, "Minimal Effects of Severe Depression on Cognitive Functioning," *Journal of Abnormal and Social Psychology* 69 (1964): 237-243. Based on a study of sixty-five normal and fifty-five depressives, depressed individuals performed more poorly by only 4 percent but rated themselves more negatively by 82 percent.

21. Lauren B. Alloy and Anthony H. Ahrens, "Depression and Pessimism for the Future: Biased Use of Statistically Relevant Information in Predictions for Self Versus Others," *Journal of Personality and Social Psychology* 41 (1987): 366-378.

22. Tom Pyszczynski and Jeff Greenberg, "Depression and Preference for Self-Focusing Stimuli Following Success and Failure," *Journal of Personality and Social Psychology* 49, no. 4 (1985): 1066-1075.

23. Michael S. Greenberg, Carmelo V. Vazquez, and Lauren B. Alloy, "Depression Versus Anxiety: Differences in Self-and Other-Schemata," in *Cognitive Processes in Depression*, ed. Lauren B. Alloy (New York: Guilford Press, 1988), 109-142.

24. Beck, *Depression*, 285.

25. Constance Hammen and Susan E. Krantz, "Effect of Success and Failure on Depressive Cognitions," *Journal of Abnormal Psychology* 85 (1976): 577-586.

26. S. D. Hollon and P. C. Kendall, "Cognitive Self-Statements in Depression: Development of an Automatic Thoughts Questionnaire," *Cognitive Therapy and Research* 4 (1980): 383-395.

27. Aaron T. Beck, Gary Brown, Robert Steer, Judy I. Eidelson, and John H. Riskind, "Differentiating Anxiety and Depression: A Test of the Cognitive Content Specificity Hypotheses," *Journal of Abnormal Psychology* 96 (1987): 179-183.

28. Carol M. Anderson, Sona Dimidjian, and Apryl Miller, "Family Therapy," in *Treating Depression*, ed. Ira D. Glick (San Francisco, CA: Jossey-Bass Publishers, 1995), 1.

29. R. Janoff-Bulman and B. Hecker, "Depression, Vulnerability, and World Assumptions," *Cognitive Processes in Depression*, ed. Lauren B. Alloy (New York: Guilford Press, 1988), 177-192.

30. James C. Coyne, "Depression and the Response of Others" *Journal of Abnormal Psychology* 85 (1976): 186-193.

31. Gotlib and Hammen, *Psychological Aspects of Depression*, 161.

32. Anderson, Dimidjian, and Miller, "Family Therapy," 3.

33. Ian H. Gotlib and S. J. Meltzer, "Depression and the Perception of Social Skill in Dyadic Interaction," *Cognitive Therapy and Research* 11 (1987): 41-53.

34. Karp, *Speaking of Sadness*, 35.

35. Ibid.

36. Lynn P. Rehm and Mary J. Naus, "A Memory Model of Emotion," in *Contemporary Psychological Approaches to Depression: Theory, Research, and Treatment*, ed. Rick E. Ingram, (New York: Plenum Press, 1990), 30.

37. Cited by Karp, *Speaking of Sadness*, 32.

38. Styron, *Darkness Visible*, 19.

39. Karp, *Speaking of Sadness*, 56.

40. Binford W. Gilbert, The Pastoral Care of Depression (Binghamton, NY: The Haworth Press, 1998), 24.

41. Hammen, "Vulnerability to Depression," 61.

42. Kuang-ming Wu, *Chuang Tzu: World Philosopher at Play* (New York: Crossroad Publishing, 1982), 91.

43. Ibid., 94.

44. Pyszczynski and Greenberg, *Hanging On and Letting Go*, 13.

45. Shelley Duval and Robert A. Wicklund, *A Theory of Objective Self-Awareness* (New York: Academic Press, 1972), 53.

46. Ibid., 54.

47. Pyszczynski and Greenberg, *Hanging On and Letting Go*, 14.

48. Duval and Wicklund, *A Theory of Objective Self-Awareness*, 2.

49. Ibid.

50. Pyszczynski and Greenberg, *Hanging On and Letting Go*, 14.

51. Pyszczynski and Greenberg, *Hanging On and Letting Go*, 14-15.

52. Andrew G. Billings and Rudolf H. Moos, "Coping, Stress, and Social Resources Among Adults with Unipolar Depression," *Journal of Personality and Social Psychology* 46 (1984): 877-891; Susan Folkman and Richard S. Lazarus, "Stress Process and Depressive Symptomatology," *Journal of Abnormal Psychology* 95 (1986): 107-113.

53. Rick E. Ingram and T. W. Smith, "Depression and Internal Versus External Focus of Attention," *Cognitive Therapy and Research* 8 (1984): 139-152.

54. Pyszczynski and Greenberg, "Depression and Preference for Self-Focusing Stimuli After Success and Failure," 1067. In supporting this theory they make reference to the following studies: Arnold H. Buss, *Self-Consciousness and Social Anxiety* (San Francisco: W. H. Freeman, 1980); Charles S. Carver and Michael F. Sheier, *Attention and Self-regulation: A Control-theory Approach to Human Behavior* (New York: Springer-Verlag, 1981); and Duval and Wicklund, *A Theory of Objective Self-Awareness*.

55. Robert Wicklund and Shelley Duval, "Opinion Change and Performance Facilitation as a Result of Objective Self-awareness," *Journal of Experimental Social Psychology* 7 (1971): 319-342.

56. Robert Wicklund and Dieter Frey, "Self-awareness Theory: When the Self Makes a Difference," in *The Self in Social Psychology*, eds. Daniel M. Wegner and Robin R. Vallacher, (New York: Oxford University Press, 1980), 31-54.

57. Tom Pyszczynski and Jeff Greenberg, "Depressive Self-Focusing Style," *Journal of Research in Personality* 20 (1986): 96.

58. Wu, *Chuang Tzu*, 94.

59. Pyszczynski and Greenberg, *Hanging On and Letting Go*, 29.

60. Ibid., 16.

61. Ibid.

62. Ibid., 28-29.

63. Ed Diener and Thomas K. Srull, "Self-awareness, Psychological Perspective, and the Self-Reinforcement in Relation to Personal and Social Standards," *Journal of Personality and Social Psychology* 37 (1979): 413-423.

64. Arthur L. Beaman, Bonnel Klentz, Edward Diener, and Soren Svanum, "Objective Self-Awareness and Transgression in Children: A Field Study," *Journal of Personality and Social Psychology* 37 (1979): 1835-1846; Edward Diener and Mark C. Wallbom, "Effects of Self-Awareness on Anti-Normative Behavior," *Journal of Research in Personality* 10 (1976): 107-111. This study reports that 71 percent of the subjects cheated on an anagram test under nonself-aware condition whereas only 7 percent cheated under self-aware condition.

65. Frederick X. Gibbons, "Sexual Standards and Reactions to Pornography: Enhancing Behavioral Consistency through Self-Focused Attention," *Journal of Personality and Social Psychology* 36 (1978): 976-987.

Chapter 5

1. Howard Stone, *Depression and Hope: New Insights for Pastoral Counseling* (Minneapolis: Fortress Press, 1998), 1.

2. Tom Pyszczynski and Jeff Greenberg, *Hanging On and Letting Go: Understanding the Onset, Progression, and Remission of Depression* (New York: Springer-Verlag, 1992), 59-60.

3. Pyszczynski and Greenberg, "Depression and Preference for Self-Focusing Stimuli After Success and Failure," 1066-1075; Tom Pyszczynski and Jeff Greenberg, "Evidence for a Depressive Self-Focusing Style," *Journal of Research in Personality* 20 (1986): 95-106.

4. Pyszczynski and Greenberg, *Hanging On and Letting Go*, 59.

5. Eddie Harmon-Jones, Linda Simon, Jeff Greenberg, Tom Pyszczynski, Sheldon Solomon, and Holly McGregor, "Terror Management Theory and Self-esteem: Evidence that Increased Self-esteem Reduces Mortality Salience Effects," *Journal of Personality and Social Psychology* 72, no. 1 (1997): 24-36. This experiment was conducted at the University of Arizona and participants included thirty-four women and fifteen men.

6. Lyn Y. Abramson, Martin E. Seligman, and John D. Teasdale, "Learned Helplessness in Humans: Critique and Reformation," *Journal of Abnormal Psy-*

chology 87 (1978): 65-66; Aaron T. Beck, *Depression: Clinical, Experimental, and Theoretical Aspects* (New York: Harper and Row, 1967).

7. Pyszczynski and Greenberg, *Hanging On and Letting Go*, 43-44.

8. Ibid., 44. The term "cultural" here refers to the collective belief about common values that are rooted in religious beliefs and worldviews.

9. Jeff Greenberg, Sheldon Solomon, Mitchell Veeder, Deborah Lyon, Tom Pyszczynski, Abram Rosenblatt, and Shari Kirkland, "Evidence for Terror Management Theory II: The Effects of Mortality Salience on Reactions to Those Who Threaten or Bolster the Cultural Worldview," *Journal of Personality and Social Psychology* 58, no. 2 (1990): 308-318.

10. Ibid., 308-318.

11. Pyszczynski and Greenberg, *Hanging On and Letting Go*, 49.

12. Ibid., 103.

13. Ibid., 79.

14. Beck, *Depression: Causes and Treatments* (Philadelphia: University of Pennsylvania Press, 1972), 24; Ian H. Gotlib and Constance L. Hammen. *Psychological Aspects of Depression: Toward a Cognitive-Interpersonal Integration* (New York: John Wiley and Sons, 1992), 3; Pyszczynski and Greenberg, *Hanging Out and Letting Go*, 79, 88.

15. Renee-Louise Franche, "Self-Critism and Dependency as Vulnerability Factors to Depression," PhD diss., University of British Columbia (Canada), 1991.

16. Beck, *Depression: Causes and Treatments*, 24.

17. Andrew G. Billings and Rudolf H. Moos, "Coping, Stress, and Social Resources Among Adults with Unipolar Depression," *Journal of Personality and Social Psychology*, 46 (1984): 877-891.

18. Pyszczynski and Greenberg, "Depression and Preference for Self-Focusing Stimuli After Success and Failure," 1067. In supporting this theory they make reference to the following studies: Arnold H. Buss, *Self-Consciousness and Social Anxiety* (San Francisco: W. H. Freeman, 1980); Charles S. Carver and Michael F. Scheier, *Attention and Self-Regulation: A Control-Theory Approach to Human Behavior* (New York: Springer-Verlag, 1981).

19. Michael F. Scheier and Charles S. Carver, "Individual Differences in Self-Concept and Self-Process," *The Self in Social Psychology*, eds Daniel. M. Wegner and Robin R. Vallacher, (New York: Oxford University Press, 1980), 229-251.

20. Pyszczynski and Greenberg, *Hanging On and Letting Go*,88.

21. Paul H. Blaney, "Affect and Memory: A Review,"*Psychological Bulletin* 99 (1986): 229-246.

22. David M. Clark and John D. Teasdale, "Diurnal Variation in clinical Depression and Accessibility of Memories of Positive and Negative Experiences," *Journal of Abnormal Psychology* 91 (1982): 87-95.

23. Tom Pyszczynski, James C. Hamilton, Fred H. Herring, and Jeff Greenberg, "Depression, Self-Focused Attention, and the Negative Memory Bias," *Journal of Personality and Social Psychology* 57 no. 2 (1989): 351-357; see also Nicholas A. Kuiper, Paul A. Derry, and Michael R. MacDonald, "Self-Reference and Person Perception in Depression: A Social Cognition Perspective," in *Integrations of Clini-*

cal and Social Psychology, eds. Gifford Weary and Herbert Mirels (New York: Oxford University Press, 1982), 79-103.

24. The scores are based on Beck Depressive Inventory. Subjects scoring 9 and above were classified as depressed while subjects scoring under 4 and below were classified as nondepressed.

25. Pyszczynski, Hamilton, Herring, and Greenberg, "Depression, Self-Focused Attention, and the Negative Memory Bias," 351-357. It is interesting to note that the study by Franche did not show correlation between negative memory bias and depression. However, the study did not induce self-focused attention and negative mood as in the study by Pyszczynski, Hamilton, Herring, Greenberg. Renee-Louise Franche, "Self-criticism and Dependency." A study similar to that of Pyszczynski, Hamilton, Herring, and Greenberg was conducted by Edward John Giaquinto to measure negative memory bias among persons who were clinically depressed. According to this study, depressed and nondepressed individuals who were manipulated to focus their attention externally, recalled more positive life events than those who were self-focused. Edward John Giaquinto Jr., "Depression, Self-focused Attention and Negative Memory Bias: A Replication and Extension," (PhD diss., California School of Professional Psychology, 1995).

26. Pyszczynski and Greenberg, "Depression and Preference for Self-Focusing Stimuli After Success and Failure," 1067. Rick E. Ingram and T. W. Smith, "Depression and Internal versus External Focus of Attention," *Cognitive Therapy and Research* 8 (1984): 139-151.

27. Pyszczynski and Greenberg, "Depression and Preference for Self-Focusing Stimuli After Success and Failure," 1066-1075. See also Jeff Greenberg, "Persistent High Self-Focus After Failure and Low Self-focus After Success: The Depressive Self-Focusing Style," *Journal of Personality and Social Psychology* 50, no. 5 (1986): 1039-44; and Pyszczynski and Greenberg, "Evidence for a Depressive Self-Focusing Style," 95-106.

28. Pyszczynski and Greenberg, "Depression and Preference for Self-Focusing Stimuli After Success and Failure," 1072.

29. Nicholas A Kuiper, "Depression and Causal Attributions for Success and Failure," *Journal of Personality and Social Psychology* 36 (1978): 236-46; Pyszczynski and Greenberg, "Depression and Preference for Self-Focusing Stimuli Following Success and Failure," 1066-75. See also Paul D. Sweeney, Karen Anderson, and Scott Bailey, "Attributional Style in Depression: A Meta-Analytic Review," *Journal of Personality and Social Psychology* 50 (1986): 974-991.

30. David A. Karp, *Speaking of Sadness: Depression, Disconnection, and the Meanings of Illness* (New York: Oxford University Press, 1996), 31.

31. Paula Ray Pietromonaco, *The Nature of the Self-structure in Depression*, PhD diss., University of Michigan, 1983, abstract in *Dissertation Abstracts International* 44-10B (1983): 3243.

32. Pyszczynski and Greenberg, *Hanging On and Letting Go*, 107.

33. Karp, *Speaking of Sadness*, 31.

34. Lao Tzu, *Tao Te Ching: A New English Version*, trans. Stephen Mitchell (New York: Harper and Row, 1988), 58.

Chapter 6

1. Lao Tzu, *The Way of Life: A New Translation of the Tao Te Ching*, trans. Raymond Bernard Blackney (New York: New American Library, 1955), 93.

2. Cited by Alan Watts, *Tao: The Watercourse Way* (New York: Pantheon Books, 1975), 38.

3. Stanley Cavell, *In Quest of the Ordinary: Lines of Skepticism and Romanticism* (Chicago: University of Chicago Press, 1988), 48.

4. Lao Tzu, *The Way of Life*, trans. Blackney, 101.

5. It is believed that Confucius visited Lao Tzu around 518 B.C., while at the same time it was believed that Lao Tzu's son served as a general in 273 B.C. Both could not possibly have been true. Chinese tradition accepted the former and placed Lao Tzu twenty years senior to Confucius. Western scholars dated Lao Tzu at the fourth or even third century B.C. Chinese scholars' opinions on the dating are evenly divided. Scholars in mainland China (since 1949) placed him in the later date. The legend that Lao Tzu never really existed but was merely a name given to three different accounts is no longer entertained by scholars. Chan Wing-tsit, comp. and trans. *A Source Book in Chinese Philosophy* (Princeton: Princeton University Press, 1963), 138.

6. Watts, *Tao*, xxii.

7. Chan, *A Source Book in Chinese Philosophy*, 136.

8. Angus Graham, trans., Introduction to *Chuang-Tzu: The Seven Inner Chapters and Other Writings from the Book Chuang-tzu* (London: George Allen and Uwin, 1982), 4-5.

9. Ibid., 36-37.

10. Watts, *Tao*, 38. *Tzu-jan* is translated "naturally, of itself."; from *Tzu*, self, and *jan*, an adverbial suffix 'ly'. It means that which happens of itself without prompting. It is spontaneous. Raymond Bernard Blackney, Introduction to *The Way of Life: A New Translation of the Tao Te Ching* by Lao-tzu (New York: New American Library, 1955), 40.

11. Chung-yuan Chang, *Creativity and Taoism: A Study of Chinese Philosophy, Art, and Poetry* (New York: Julian Press, 1963), 32.

12. Chuang Tzu, *Chuang Tzu: Basic Writings*, trans. Burton Watson (New York: Columbia University Press, 1996), 36.

13. Chan, *A Source Book in Chinese Philosophy*, 182.

14. Chuang-Tzu, *The Texts of Taoism*, trans. James Legge (New York: Julian Press, 1959), 506.

15. Lao Tzu, *Tao Te Ching*, trans. Mitchell, 11.

16. Ibid., 66.

17. Wayne D. Owens, "Tao and Difference: The Existential Implications," *Journal of Chinese Philosophy* 20 (1993): 275.

18. In discussing the freedom of being which emerges from non-being, Chenyang Li contrasted Chuang Tzu's concept of being to that of Aristotle who believed that an object only has one essence and one primary being. To Chuang Tzu there is no "single objectively correct answer to the question of what an object is." A being is both a

"this" and a "that" at the same time. Chenyang Li, "What-Being: Chuang Tzu versus Aristotle," *International Philosophical Quarterly* 33, no. 3 (1993): 341-353.

19. Max Kaltenmark, *Lao Tzu and Taoism*, trans. Roger Greaves (Stanford: Stanford University Press, 1969), 55.

20. Kaltenmark translates *wu wei* as "without doing" or "absence of action." Ibid., 53; Ownes renders this term, "non-purposive action or participation without manipulation." Ownes, 270; to Wu it means "trying that is no trying." Kuang-ming Wu, *Chuang Tzu; World Philosopher at Play* (New York: Crossroad Publishing, 1982), 91.

21. Daisetz Teitaro Suzuki, Introduction to *The Text of Taoism*, trans. James Legge (New York: Julian Press, 1959), 24.

22. Chuang Tzu, *Wandering on the Way: Early Taoist Tales and Parables of Chuang Tzu*, trans. Victor H. Mair (Honolulu: University of Hawaii Press, 1994), 26-27.

23. Kaltenmark, *Lao Tzu and Taoism*, 53.

24. Margaret Chatterjee, *The Existentialist Outlook* (New Delhi: Orient Longman, 1973), 137. This concept of *dasein* aims also at resolving the subject-object dichotomy of Kant. The nonexistence of this dichotomy becomes more obvious in Jean Paul Sartre's analysis of consciousness. Consciousness arises only in relation to objects outside of itself. There is no consciousness-in-itself apart from other objects; in fact, consciousness cannot arise without an external object. Thus consciousness is nothingness. It is nothing in itself because consciousness is always consciousness of something or someone. Therefore, if being can become conscious of itself only in relation to objects, the question of the dichotomy does not exist as such. Jean Paul Sartre, *Being and Nothingness: A Phenomenological Essay on Ontology*, trans. Hazel E. Barnes (New York: Washington Square Press, 1956).

25. Marjorie Green, "Heidegger, Martin,"in *The Encyclopedia of Philosophy*, vol. 3, ed. Paul Edwards (New York: Macmillan Publishing, 1967), 459-465; see also Dietrich Bonhoeffer, *Act and Being*, trans. Bernard Noble (New York: Harper and Row, 1961), 51-53.

26. Bonhoeffer, *Act and Being*, 51.

27. Green, "Heidigger, Martin," 461.

28. Ibid.

29. John Macquarrie, *Existentialism* (Middlesex, England: Penguin Books, 1972), 189-205.

30. For Chuang Tzu's discussion on the meaning of "this" and "that" see Victor H. Mair, trans. *Wandering On the Way: Early Taoist Tales and Parables of Chuang Tzu* (Honolulu: University of Hawaii Press, 1994),15.

31. Carl Jung, *The Undiscovered Self* (Boston: Little, Brown, 1958), 92. Speaking of consciousness Fukunaga believes that consciousness is one of the main obstacles because it sets up abstract categories and intellectual divisions. Livia Kohn, *Early Chinese Mysticism: Philosophy and Soteriology in the Taoist Tradition* (Princeton: Princeton University Press, 1992), 54. Suzuki equates the state of unconscious to the innocence of life in the garden of Eden and believes that we are still in this Garden and, hence, this level of unconsciousness (not being conscious of our doing and

the knowledge of good and evil) is still attainable. Suzuki, Introduction to *The Text of Taoism,* 29-30.

32. Kohn, *Early Chinese Mysticism,* 48.

33. Carl Jung, *The Undiscovered Self* (Boston: Little, Brown, 1958), 75. When we attempt to fit life into logic, we create conflict within ourselves because life is greater than logic.

34. A moral issue is being raised here too. If there is no right and wrong, what is morality? Chuang Tzu's discussion on right and wrong is not within the context of morality. He is concerned with the motive behind the pursuit of right and wrong.

35. Lao Tzu, *Tao Te Ching,* trans. Mitchell, 37.

36. Wu, *Chuang Tzu,* 63.

37. Lao Tzu, *Tao Te Ching,* trans. Mitchell, 48.

38. Burton Watson, trans. Introduction to *Chuang Tzu: Basic Writings* by Burton Watson (New York: Columbia University Press, 1996), 6.

39. Masao Abe, *Zen and Comparative Studies,* ed. Steven Heine (Honolulu: University of Hawaii, 1997), 33.

40. Jung Young Lee, *The Trinity in Asian Perspective* (Nashville: Abingdon Press, 1996), 31.

41. Wu, *Chuang Tzu,* 64.

42. Ibid., 80.

43. This concept resonates with the existentialist's formula "existence precedes essence." Since being comes from nothing, there is no predefined formula of what this being ought to be. Essence must be created. Being is possibility and destiny is to be created out of nothing. Macquarrie, *Existentialism,* 61-78.

44. Li, "What Being," 352.

45. Watts, *Tao,* 96.

Chapter 7

1. Kuang-ming Wu, *Chuang Tzu; World Philosopher at Play* (New York: Crossroad Publishing, 1982), 91.

2. Ibid.

3. These two selves reflect two functions of the self and its essence.

4. Wu, *Chuang Tzu,* 94.

5. Ibid.

6. Victor H. Mair, trans. *Wandering On the Way: Early Taoist Tales and Parables of Chuang Tzu* (Honolulu: University of Hawaii Press, 1994), 76.

7. Ibid., 75.

8. An ethical question arises when we hear Chuang Tzu's advice that moral individuals should not take corrective measures when confronted with evil in society. The question becomes more accentuated when we hear his comments that moral correction does violence to the natural way. Do we have moral responsibility when we face evil within our society? There are two answers to this question. First, the natural way here embraces *yin* and *yang. Wu wei* aims at this balance. If *wu wei* aims at this balance there is therefore no extreme evil within the society. The extreme of

evil is viewed, according to Chuang Tzu and Lao Tzu, as a result of the denial of the existence of *yin* and *yang*. In such a denial we pursue the one without acknowledging the other. In such a pursuit one reinforces the movement to an extreme. The extreme pursuit of *yin* lands one in the *yang*. The extreme pursuit of righteousness evokes greater inclination toward sin and immorality.

9. Chuang Tzu, *Chuang Tzu: Basic Writings*. trans. Burton Watson (New York: Columbia University Press, 1996), 39.

10. Wu, *Chuang Tzu*, 94.

11. Chuang Tzu, *The Texts of Taoism: The Tao Te Ching, The Writings of Chuang-Tzu and the Thai-Shang*, trans. James Legge and intro. Daisetz Teitaro Suzuki (New York: Julian Press, 1959), 456.

12. Wu, *Chuang Tzu*, 94.

13. Are not there people who try hard to the best of their ability and feel great accomplishing their goals, one may ask. This is true. However, if that goal becomes a standard whereby one judges one's value, one may be trapped in its power to define one's worth.

14. David A. Karp. *Speaking of Sadness: Depression, Disconnection, and the Meaning of Illness* (New York: Oxford University Press, 1996), 29.

15. Wu, *Chuang Tzu*, 95.

16. Ibid.

17. Ibid.

18. Ibid., 97

19. Ibid., 98.

20. Chuang Tzu, *Chuang Tzu*, trans. Watson, 40.

21. Cited by Wu, *Chuang Tzu*, 98.

22. Ibid., 104. This concept is reflected in Tillich's analysis of human beings in relation to the world. Ontology occupies a prominent place in the life of human beings. As human beings we ask ontological questions and come to realize that the answers are implied in this very being itself. The answer is contained in "being" because this ontological structure is there a priori. Paul Tillich, *Systematic Theology*, vol. 1, (London: SCM Press, 1951-1957), 168.

23. The concept of *wu wei* as a way out by moving away from distinction is similar with Heidegger's concept of releasement. Releasement allows one to step out of the realm of distinction and let the self just be. It remains open to possibility. Here the self keeps oneself open to the phenomenon without having anything definite in mind. Joan Stambaugh, "Heidegger, Taoism, and the Question of Metaphysics," in *Heidegger and Asian Thought*, ed. Graham Parkes (Honolulu: University of Hawaii Press, 1987), 85-87.

24. Wu, *Chuang Tzu*, 98. Or, in the language of self-regulatory perseveration, the more self-focused one becomes, the more aware one will be of the discrepancy. The heightened awareness leads the self to regulate itself as an attempt to reduce the gap.

25. Tillich, *Systematic Theology*, vol. 1, 186-198.

26. Dietrich Bonhoeffer, *Ethics*, ed. Eberhard Bethge, trans. Neville Horton Smith (New York: Macmillan, 1955), 1.

27. Dietrich Bonhoeffer, *Creation and Fall: Temptation*, trans. John Fletcher and Kathleen Downham (New York: Macmillan, 1959), 51.

28. Wu, *Chuang Tzu*, 100.

29. Harold I. Kaplan, Benjamin J. Sadock, and Jack A. Grebb, *Kaplan and Sadock's Synopsis of Psychiatry: Behavioral Sciences, Clinical Psychiatry,* Seventh Edition (Baltimore: Williams and Wilkins, 1994), 82-83; see also Melody Beattie, *Codependent No More: How to Stop Controlling Others and Start Caring for Yourself* (New York: Harper and Row, 1987), 126-127.

30. Lao Tzu. *Tao Te Ching: A New English Version,* trans. Stephen Mitchell (New York: Harper and Row, 1988), 38.

31. Chuang Tzu, *The Texts of Taoism: The Tao Te Ching, The Writings of Chuang-Tzu and the Thai-Shang,* trans. James Legge and intro. Daisetz Teitaro Suzuki (New York: Julian Press, 1959), 339.

32. Wu, *Chuang Tzu*, 100-102.

33. Ibid., 106-109.

34. Masao Abe, *Zen and Comparative Studies,* ed. Steven Heine (Honolulu: University of Hawaii Press, 1997), 33.

35. Mair, *Wandering on the Way,* 71.

36. In explaining the concept of *anatta* or *anatman,* Fedor Ippolitovich Stcherbatsky, a Buddhist scholar, uses the term radical pluralism as a context. Elements alone are real. Every combination of these elements are mere names for the plurality of separate elements. Existence as a whole is an interplay of a plurality of subtle but unanalyzable basic elements. This interplay of unanalyzable elements is governed by an impersonal, transcendental law that is not accessible to human intellect. Reality belongs only to the basic elements. Any combination of these elements is impermanent. Every impermanent combination moves through the cycle of combination and separation of basic elements. This cycle implies suffering. This is the basic understanding of the doctrine of *anatta* because *atman* or self, "is a mere name for a multitude of interconnected facts, which Buddhist philosophy is attempting to analyze by reducing them to real elements." Fedor Ippolitovich Stcherbatsky, *The Central Conception of Buddhism* (New Delhi: Motilal Banarsidass, 1922), 25.

37. Wu, *Chuang Tzu*, 103.

38. Abe, *Zen and Comparative Studies,* 31.

39. Chuang Tzu, *Chuang Tzu,* trans. Watson, 72.

Chapter 8

1. Thomas Moore, *Care of the Soul: A Guide for Cultivating Depth and Sacredness in Everyday Life* (New York: HarperPerrenial, 1992), 19.

2. Seward Hiltner, *Preface to Pastoral Theology* (Nashville: Abingdon, 1958), 89-174.

3. Liston O. Mills, "Pastoral Care: History, Tradition, and Definitions." In *Dictionary of Pastoral Care and Counseling,* ed. Rodney J. Hunter, 836-844 (Nashville: Abingdon Press, 1990), 836-837.

4. LeRoy Aden, "Comfort/Sustaining," in *Dictionary of Pastoral Care and Counseling,* ed. Rodney J. Hunter (Nashville: Abingdon, 1990), 193.

5. Ibid., 194.

6. William Styron, *Darkness Visible: A Memoir of Madness* (New York: Vintage Books, 1990), 56.

7. Ian H. Gotlib and Constance L. Hammen, *Psychological Aspects of Depression: Toward a Cognitive-Interpersonal Integration* (New York: John Wiley and Sons, 1992), 257.

8. Tom Pyszczynski and Jeff Greenberg, *Hanging On and Letting Go: Understanding the Onset, Progression, and Remission of Depression* (New York: Springer-Verlag, 1992), 62. Studies of the concept of self-complexity by Patricia W. Linville show that the more complex one's self-concept is, the less vulnerable one becomes when faced with distress in life. This is because the self has a complex system of assessing its worth. Patricia W. Linville, "Self-Complexity As a Cognitive Buffer Against Stress-Related Illness and Depression," *Journal of Personality and Social Psychology* 52 (1987): 663-676.

9. Pyszczynski and Greenberg, *Hanging On and Letting Go,* 118.

10. David Rosen, *Transforming Depression: Healing the Soul Through Creativity* (New York: Penguin Books, 1993), 61-84. Rosen offers three stages in the healing journey through egocide. In the first stage, one works through complexes with one's parents and through analysis comes to identify negative introjects (negative mother and father complexes). Once identified, an individual will have to get rid of these negative introjects ("kill" these introjects which one has been identifying with one's ego-image by articulating or analyzing until these introjects have no power over oneself). In the second stage, one usually feels dead since ego-identity is dead. One becomes anxious and confused. Through therapeutic alliance, the ego-self slowly emerges. In the final stage, the self (the ego or the center of consciousness) will move toward the self (the totality of psyche emcompassing the conscious and the unconscious) where there is the union of the opposites. One works on ending therapy and finding one's own path. Ibid., 77-80.

11. Søren Kierkegaard, *The Journals of Kierkegaard,* ed. Alexander Dru (New York: Harper and Row, 1958), 127-128.

12. Pyszczynski and Greenberg, *Hanging On and Letting Go,* 127.

13. Ibid., 129.

14. See Joan V. Wood, Judith A. Saltzberg, John M. Neale, Arthur A. Stone, and Tracy B. Rachmiel, "Self-focused Attention, Coping Responses, and Distressed Mood in Everyday Life," *Journal of Personality and Social Psychology* 58, no. 6 (1990): 1027-1036; Renee-Louise Franche, "Self-criticism and Dependency as Vulnerability Factors to Depression," PhD diss., University of British Columbia, 1991.

15. Pyszczynski and Greenberg, *Hanging On and Letting Go,* 114.

16. Edward John Giaquinto Jr., "Depression, Self-Focused Attention and Negative Memory Bias: A Replication and Extension," PhD diss, California School of Professional Psychology (San Diego), 1995.

17. Pyszczynski and Greenberg, *Hanging On and Letting Go,* 126.

18. Chuang Tzu, *Chuang Tzu: Basic Writings,* trans. Burton Watson (New York: Columbia University Press, 1996), 42.

19. Kuang-ming Wu, *Chuang Tzu: World Philosopher at Play* (New York: Crossroad Publishing, 1982), 64.

20. John Stambaugh, "Heidegger, Taoism, and the Question of Metaphysics." In *Heidegger and Asian Thought,* ed. Graham Parkes, 79-91 (Honolulu: University of Hawaii Press, 1987), 89.

21. Lao *Tzu. Tao Te Ching: A New English Version,* trans. Stephen Mitchell (New York: Harper and Row, 1988), 63.

22. John James Clarke, *In Search of Jung: Historical and Philosophical Enquiries* (London: Routledge, 1992), 125; see also Edward Edinger, *Ego and Archetype: Individuation and the Religious Function of the Psyche* (Baltimore: Penguin, 1972), 130.

23. Søren Kierkegaard, *Fear and Trembling: Sickness Unto Death,* Walter Lowrie (Princeton: Princeton University Press, 1954), 150-151.

24. Dietrich Bonhoeffer, *Ethics,* ed. Eberhard Bethge, trans. Neville Horton Smith (New York: Macmillan, 1955), 27.

25. Moore, *Care of the Soul,* 146.

26. Ibid., 154.

27. Keiji Nishitani, a Japanese philosopher of the Kyoto School, uses the term "nihility" to refer to this process. Nihility is that which makes meaningless the meaning of life. It occurs when we question our very own existence. Yet it is this very nihility that invites us to return to life again. This nothingness is the place where one may rediscover the meaning of life. Keiji Nishitani, *Religion and Nothingness,* trans. Jan Van Bragt (Berkeley, CA: University of California Press, 1982), 4.

28. Pyszczynski and Greenberg, *Hanging On and Letting Go,* 62.

29. Moore also identifies this process with depression. Moore, *Care of the Soul,* 139.

30. Masao Abe, Zen and Comparative Studies. ed. Steven Heine (Honolulu: University of Hawaii Press, 1997), 33.

31. Moore, *Care of the Soul,* 9.

32. Ibid.

33. Alan Watts, *Tao: The Watercourse Way* (New York: Pantheon Books, 1963), 88.

34. Raimundo Panikkar, *Myth, Faith, and Hermeneutics: Cross-Cultural Studies* (New York: Paulist, 1979), 264.

35. Choan Seng Song, *Theology from the Womb of Asia* (Maryknoll, NY: Orbis Books, 1986), 207.

36. Jung, *The Portable Jung,* trans. R. F. C. Hall (New York: Penguin Books, 1971), 1441-1448. Shadows refer to the dark aspects of our personality that we perceive as unacceptable. Because we perceive them as unacceptable, they remain at the unconscious level and are not integrated into the total personality.

Chapter 9

1. Carl Jung, *Psychology and Western Religion,* trans. R. f. C. Hull (New Jersey: Princeton University Press, 1984), 198-199.

2. Masao Abe, *Zen and Comparative Studies,* ed. Steven Heine (Honolulu: University of Hawaii Press, 1997), 35.

3. Richard Rohr, *Simplicity: the Art of Living*, trans. Peter Heinegg (New York: Crossroad Publishing, 1991), 21.

4. Ibid., 165.

5. Lao Tzu, *The Way of Life According to Laotzu*, trans. Witter Bynner (New York: The John Day Company, 1944, 51-52).

6. Rohr, *Simplicity*, 165.

7. Thomas Moore, *Care of the Soul: A Guide for Cultivating Depth and Sacredness in Everyday Life* (New York: HarperPerrenial, 1992), xix.

8. Rohr, *Simplicity*, 180.

9. Greg Johanson and Ron Kurtz, *Grace Unfolding: Psychotherapy in the Spirit of the Tao-Te Ching* (New York: Bell Tower, 1991), 12.

10. Ibid., 12.

11. Ibid., 5.

12. Howard Stone, *Depression and Hope: New Insights for Pastoral Counseling* (Minneapolis: Fortress Press, 1998), 32.

13. For more information on how to help suicidal individuals see Stone's "Suicide and Depression," in Ibid., 32-38. See also John H. Hewett, "Suicide Prevention," in *Dictionary of Pastoral Care and Counseling*, ed. Rodney J. Hunter (Nashville, Abingdon Press, 1990), 1235-1237.

14. James Hillman, *The Soul's Code: In Search of Character and Calling* (New York: Warner Books, 1997), 12.

15. Johanson and Kurtz, *Grace Unfolding*, 56.

16. Edwin Friedman, "Bowen Theory and Therapy," in *Handbook of Family Therapy*, vol 2, eds. Alan S. Gurman and David P. Kniskern (New York: Brunner/Mazel, 1991), 161.

17. For further discussion on meditation from Eastern perspective, see David Brazier, *Zen Therapy: Transcending the Sorrows of the Human Mind* (New York: John Wiley and Sons, 1995), 64-73 and 138-142.

18. Victor H. Mair, trans., *Wandering On the Way: Early Taoist Tales and parables of Chuang Tzu* (Honolulu: University of Hawaii Press, 1994), 75.

19. Hillman, *The Soul's Code*, 30.

20. Johanson and Kurtz, *Grace Unfolding*, 100.

21. Friedman, "Bowen Theory and Therapy," 161.

Chapter 10

1. David A. Karp, *Speaking of Sadness: Depression, Disconnection, and the Meaning of Illness* (New York: Oxford University Press, 1996), 191.

2. Siroj Sorajjakool, reflection on clinical pastoral education experience, Loma Linda University Medical Center, Calif., June 28, 1996.

3. Paul Tillich, *Courage to Be* (Glasgov: Collins, 1957), 41-42.

4. Kuang-ming Wu, *Chuang Tzu: World Philosopher at Play* (New York: Crossroad Publishing, 1982), 64. Although Tillich recognizes the importance of nonbeing and places it at the foundation of ontology, his system still recognizes the priority of being over non-being. Ibid., 41.

5. Wing-tsit Chan, com. and trans., *A Source Book in Chinese Philosophy, Art, and Poetry* (New York: Julian Press, 1963), 316.

6. Lao Tzu, *The Way of Life According to Laotzu*, trans. Witter Bynner (New York: The John Day Company, 1944), 30-31.

7. Alan Watts, *Tao: The Watercourse Way* (New York: Pantheon Books, 1963), 19-28. See also Jung Young Lee's explanation of the concept of *I-Ching* (the *Book of Changes*). Jung Young Lee, *The Trinity in Asian Perspective* (Nashville: Abingdon Press, 1996), 24-35.

8. Lee, *The Trinity in Asian Perspective*, 31.

9. Tillich believes these factors can also drive us into our selfishness and self-preoccupation. Tillich employs the term concupiscence to describe this state. Concupiscence refers to the gratification of our instinctive desire which includes sex and hunger while disregarding the moral implications and results from, according to Tillich, our inability to maintain tension within ourselves. Paul Tillich, *Systematic Theology*, vol. 2 (Chicago: Chicago University Press, 1957), 51-55.

10. For further explanation on this concept see the section on "Existential Self-destruction and the Doctrine of Evil" in Paul Tillich's *Systematic Theology*, vol. 2, 59-78.

11. Margaret Chatterjee, *The Existentialist Outlook* (New Delhi: Orient Longman, 1973), 137. This concept of *dasein* aims also at resolving the subject-object dichotomy of Kant. The non-existence of this dichotomy becomes more obvious in Sartre's analysis of consciousness. Consciousness arises only in relation to objects outside of itself. There is no consciousness-in-itself apart from other objects; in fact, consciousness cannot arise without external objects. Thus consciousness is nothingness. It is nothing in itself because consciousness is always consciousness of something or someone. Therefore if being can become conscious of itself only in relation to objects, the question of the dichotomy does not exist as such. Jean Paul Sartre, *Being and Nothingness: A Phenomenological Essay on Ontology*, trans. Hazel E. Barnes (New York: Washington Square Press, 1956).

12. Marjorie Grene, "Heidegger, Martin," in *The Encyclopedia of Philosophy*, vol. 3, ed. Paul Edwards (New York: Macmillan Publishing, 1967) 459-465; see also Dietrich Bonhoeffer, *Act and Being*, trans. Bernard Noble (New York: Harper and Row, 1961), 51-53.

13. Grene, "Heidegger, Martin," 461.

14. Ibid., 463. For further discussion on the later writings of Heidegger in relation to Taoism see John Stambaugh, "Heidegger, Taoism, and the Question of Metaphysics." In *Heidegger and Asian Thought*, ed. Graham Parkes (Honolulu: University of Hawaii Press, 1987), 79-91.

15. Tillich, *Systematic Theology*, vol. 1, 186-198.

16. Dietrich Bonhoeffer, *Creation and Fall: Temptation*. trans. John Fletcher and Kathleen Downham (New York: Macmillan, 1959), 51.

17. Ibid., 52.

18. Ibid., 53.

19. Lao Tzu, *The Wisdom of Laotse*, trans. with intro. Lin Yutang (New York: The Modern Library, 1948), 41.

20. Masao Abe, *Zen and Comparative Studies,* ed. Steven Heine (Honolulu: University of Hawaii Press, 1997), 25.

21. Raimundo Panikkar, *Myth, Faith, and Hermeneutics: Cross-Cultural Studies* (New York: Paulist Press, 1979), 265.

22. Dietrich Bonhoeffer, *Letters and Papers from Prison,* ed. Eberhard Bethge (New York: Macmillan, 1971), 369-370.

23. Thomas Moore, *Care of the Soul: A Guide for Cultivating Depth and Sacredness in Everyday Life* (New York: HarperPerennial, 1992), 258.

24. Richard Bernstein, *Beyond Objectivism and Relativism: Science, Hermeneutics, and Praxis* (Philadelphia: University of Pennsylvania Press, 1983), 18.

25. Greg Johanson and Ron Kurtz, *Grace Unfolding: Psychotherapy in the Spirit of the Tao-Te Ching* (New York: Bell Tower, 1991), 61.

Bibliography

Books

Abe, Masao. *Zen and Comparative Studies.* Ed. Steven Heine. Honolulu: University of Hawaii Press, 1997.

Aden, LeRoy. "Comfort/Sustaining." In *Dictionary of Pastoral Care and Counseling,* ed. Rodney J. Hunter, 193-195. Nashville: Abingdon, 1990.

Alloy, Lauren B., Jeanne S. Albright, Lyn Y. Abramson, Lyn, and Benjamin M. Dykman. "Depressive Realism and Nondepressive Optimistic Illusions: The Role of the Self." In *Contemporary Psychological Approaches to Depression: Theory, Research, and Treatment,* ed. Rick E. Ingram, 71-86. New York: Plenum Press, 1990.

American Psychiatric Association. *Diagnostic and Statistical Manual of Mental Disorders:* (DSM-IV), Fourth Edition. Washington DC: American Psychiatric Association, 1994.

Anderson, Carol M., Sona Dimidjian, and Apryl Miller. "Family Therapy." In *Treating Depression,* ed. Ira D. Glick, 1-32. San Francisco, CA: Jossey-Bass Publishers, 1995.

Beattie, Melody. *Codependent No More: How to Stop Controlling Others and Start Caring for Yourself.* New York: Harper and Row, 1987.

Beck, Aaron T. *Depression: Causes and Treatments.* Philadelphia: University of Pennsylvania Press, 1972.

Berndt, David J. "Inventories and Scales." In *Depressive Disorders: Facts, Theories, and Treatment Methods,* eds. Benjamin B. Wolman and George Stricker, 255-274. New York: John Wiley and Sons, 1990.

Bernstein, Richard. *Beyond Objectivism and Relativism: Science, Hermeneutics and Praxis.* Philadelphia: University of Pennsylvania Press, 1983.

Billings, Andrew G., and Rudolf H. Moos. "Psychosocial Stressors, Coping, and Depression." In *Handbook of Depression: Treatment, Assessment, and Research,* eds. Ernest Beckham and William Leber, 940-974. Homewood, IL: Dorsey Press, 1985.

Blackney, Raymond Bernard. Introduction to *The Way of Life: A New Translation of the Tao Te Ching* by Lao-tzu. New York: New American Library, 1955.

Blazer, Dan G. *Depression in Late Life.* St. Louise, MA: Mosby, 1993.

Bonhoeffer, Dietrich. *Act and Being.* Trans. Bernard Noble. New York: Harper and Row, 1961.

_____. *Creation and Fall: Temptation.* Trans. John Fletcher and Kathleen Downham. New York: Macmillan, 1959.

_____. *Ethics.* Ed. Eberhard Bethge. Trans. Neville Horton Smith. New York: Macmillan, 1955.

_____. *Letters and Papers from Prison.* New York: Macmillan, 1971.

Bourne, Edmund J. *The Anxiety and Phobia Workbook.* Oakland, CA: New Harbinger Publications, 1990.

Brazier, David. *Zen Therapy: Transcending the Sorrows of the Human Mind.* New York: John Wiley and Sons, 1995.

Brown, George W., and Tirril Harris. *Social Origins of Depression: A Study of Psychiatric Disorder in Women.* London: Free Press, 1978.

Buchsbaum, Monte S., H. H. Holcomb, L. DeLisi and E. Hazlett. "Brain Imaging in Affective Disorders." In *Depression: Basic Mechanisms, Diagnosis, and Treatment,* eds. A. John Rush and Kenneth Z. Altshuler, 126-142. New York: Guilford Press, 1986.

Buss, Arnold H. *Self-Consciousness and Social Anxiety.* San Francisco: W. H. Freeman, 1980.

Carver, Charles S., and Michael F. Sheier. *Attention and Self-Regulation: A Control-theory Approach to Human Behavior.* New York: Springer-Verlag, 1981.

Cavell, Stanley. *In Quest of the Ordinary: Lines of Skepticism and Romanticism.* Chicago: University of Chicago Press, 1988.

Chan, Wing-tsit, Comp. and Trans. *A Source Book in Chinese Philosophy.* Princeton: Princeton University Press, 1963.

Chang, Chung-yuan. *Creativity and Taoism: A Study of Chinese Philosophy, Art, and Poetry.* New York: Julian Press, 1963.

Chatterjee, Margaret. *The Existentialist Outlook.* New Delhi: Orient Longman, 1973.

Chuang Tzu. *Chuang Tzu: Basic Writings.* Trans. Burton Watson. New York: Columbia University Press, 1996.

_____. *Chuang Tzu: The Seven Inner Chapters and Other Writings from the Book Chuang-Tzu.* Trans. Angus Charles Graham. London: George Allen and Unwin, 1981.

Clarke, John James. *In Search of Jung: Historical and Philosophical Enquiries.* London: Routledge, 1992.

Clayton, Paula J. "Prevalence and Course of Affective Disorders." In *Depression: Basic Mechanisms, Diagnosis, and Treatment,* eds. A. John Rush and Kenneth. Z. Altshuler, 32-44. New York: Guilford Press, 1986.

Dayringer, Richard. *Dealing with Depression: Five Pastoral Interventions.* Binghamton, NY: The Haworth Pastoral Press, 1995.

Dayringer, Richard, and Myron C. Madden. "Pastoral Counseling Dealing with Depression." In *Dealing with Depression: Five Pastoral Interventions,* ed. Richard Dayringer, 27-40. Binghamton, NY: The Haworth Pastoral Press, 1995.

Dohrenwend, Barbara, P. E. Shrout, B. Link, J. Martin, and A Skodol. "Overview and Initial Results from a Risk-factor Study of Depression and Schizophrenia." In *Mental Disorders in the Community: Progress and Challenges,* ed. J. E. Barrett, New York: Guilford Press, 1986.

Dunlap, Susan J. *Counseling Depressed Women.* Louisville: Westminster John Knox Press, 1997.

Duval, Shelley and Robert Wicklund. *A Theory of Objective Self-Awareness.* New York: Academic Press, 1972.

Fairchild, Roy W. "Sadness and Depression." In *Dictionary of Pastoral Care and Counseling,* ed. Rodney J. Hunter, 1103-1106. Nashville: Abingdon Press, 1990.

Freden, Lars. *Psychosocial Aspects of Depression: No Way Out?* Chichester, New York: John Wiley and Sons, 1982.

Freud, Sigmund. *The Freud Reader.* Ed. Peter Gay. New York: W. W. Norton, 1989.

Friedman, Edwin H. "Bowen Theory and Therapy." In *Handbook of Family Therapy,* eds. Alan S. Gurman and David P. Kniskern, 134-170. Vol. 2. New York: Brunner/Mazel, 1991.

Gilbert, Binford W. *The Pastoral Care of Depression: A Guidebook.* Binghamton, NY: The Haworth Press, 1998.

Gilman, Sid, and Sarah W. Newman. *Manter and Gatz's Essentials of Clinical Neuroanatomy and Neurophysiology,* Eighth Edition. Philadelphia: F.A. Davis, 1992.

Gotlib, Ian H., and Catherine A. Colby. *Treatment of Depression: An Interpersonal Systems Approach.* New York: Pergamon Press, 1987.

Gotlib, Ian H., and Constance L. Hammen. *Psychological Aspects of Depression: Toward a Cognitive-Interpersonal Integration.* New York: John Wiley and Sons, 1992.

Graham, Angus Charles, trans. Introduction to *Chuang-Tzu: The Seven Inner Chapters and Other Writings from the Book Chuang-Tzu,* by Angus C. Graham. London: George Allen and Unwin, 1981.

Greenberg, Michael S., Carmelo V. Vazquez, and Lauren B. Alloy. "Depression versus Anxiety: Differences in Self-and Other-Schemata." In *Cognitive Processes in Depression,* ed. Lauren B. Alloy, 109-142. New York: Guilford Press, 1988.

Grene, Marjorie. "Heidegger, Martin." In *The Encyclopedia of Philosophy,* Vol. 3, ed. Paul Edwards, 459-465. New York: Macmillan Publishing, 1967.

Grimm, George. *The Doctrine of the Buddha.* Delhi: Motilal Banarsidass, 1958.

Hammen, Constance. "Vulnerability to Depression: Personal, Situational, and Family Aspects." In *Contemporary Psychological Approaches to Depression: Theory, Research, and Treatment,* ed. Rick E. Ingram, 59-69. New York: Plenum Press, 1990.

Hedaya, Robert J. *Understanding Biological Psychiatry.* New York: W. W. Norton, 1996.

Henderson, S., D. G. Byrne, and P. Duncan-Jones. *Neurosis and the Social Environment.* New York: Academic Press, 1981.

Hewett, John H. "Suicide Prevention." In *Dictionary of Pastoral Care and Counseling,* ed. Rodney J. Hunter, 1235-1237. Nashville, Abingdon Press, 1990.

Hillman, James. *The Soul's Code: In Search of Character and Calling.* New York: Warner Books, 1997.

Hiltner, Seward. *Preface to Pastoral Theology.* Nashville: Abingdon, 1958.

Holifield, Brooks E. *A History of Pastoral Care in America: From Salvation to Self-Realization.* Nashville: Abingdon Press, 1983.

Janoff-Bulman, R., and B. Hecker. "Depression, Vulnerability, and World Assumptions." In *Cognitive Processes in Depression,* ed. Lauren B. Alloy, 177-192. New York: Guilford Press, 1988.

Janowsky, David J., and S. Craig Risch. "Adrenergic-Cholinergic Balance and Affective Disorders." In *Depression: Basic Mechanisms, Diagnosis, and Treatment,* eds. A. John Rush and Kenneth Z. Altshuler, 84-101. New York: Guilford Press, 1986.

Johanson, Greg, and Ron Kurtz. *Grace Unfolding: Psychotherapy in the Spirit of the Tao-Te Ching.* New York: Bell Tower, 1991.

Jung, Carl G. *Portable Jung.* Ed. Joseph Campbell. Trans. R. F. C. Hull. New York: Penguin Books, 1971.

_____. *Psychology and Western Religion.* Trans. R. F. C. Hull. Princeton: Princeton University Press, 1984.

_____. *The Undiscovered Self.* Trans. R. F. C. Hull. Boston: Little, Brown, 1958.

Kaltenmark, Max. *Lao Tzu and Taoism.* Trans. Roger Greaves. Stanford: Stanford University Press, 1969.

Kaplan, Harold I., Benjamin J. Sadock, and Jack A. Grebb. *Kaplan and Sadock's Synopsis of Psychiatry: Behavioral Sciences, Clinical Psychiatry,* Seventh Edition. Baltimore: Williams and Wilkins, 1994.

Karp, David A. *Speaking of Sadness: Depression, Disconnection, and the Meanings of Illness.* New York: Oxford University Press, 1996.

Kierkegaard, Søren. *Fear and Trembling; Sickness unto Death.* Trans. Walter Lowrie. Princeton: Princeton University Press, 1954.

_____. *The Journals of Kierkegaard.* Ed. Alexander Dru. New York: Harper and Row, 1958.

Koenig, Harold. "Religion and Health in Later life." In *Aging, Spirituality and Religion,* eds. M. A. Kimble, S. H. McFadden, J. W. Ellor, and J. J. Seeber, 9-29. Minneapolis: Fortress, 1995.

Kohn, Livia. *Early Chinese Mysticism: Philosophy and Soteriology in the Taoist Tradition.* Princeton: Princeton University Press, 1992.

Lao Tzu. *Tao Te Ching: A New English Version.* Trans. Stephen Mitchell. New York: Harper and Row, 1988.

_____. *The Way of Life: A New Translation of the Tao Te Ching.* Trans. Raymond B. Blackney. New York: New American Library, 1955.

_____. *The Way of Life According to Laotzu.* Trans. Witter Bynner. New York: The John Day Company, 1944.

_____. *The Wisdom of Laotse.* Trans. and ed. LinYutang. New York: The Modern Library, 1948.

Lazarus, Richard S., and Susan Folkman. *Stress, Appraisal, and Coping.* New York: Springer Verlag, 1984.

Lee, Jung Young. *The Trinity in Asian Perspective.* Nashville: Abingdon Press, 1996.

Legge, James, Trans. *The Texts of Taoism: The Tao Te Ching, The Writings of Chuang-Tzu and the Thai-Shang.* Introduction by Daisetz T. Suzuki. New York: Julian Press, 1959.

Luther, Martin. *Luther's Works,* Vol. 33, eds. Philip S. Watson and Helmut T. Lehmann. Philadelphia: Fortress Press, 1972.

Macquarrie, John. *Existentialism.* Middlesex, England: Penguin Books, 1972.

Mair, Victor H., Trans. *Wandering on the Way: Early Taoist Tales and Parables of Chuang Tzu.* Honolulu: University of Hawaii Press, 1994.

Mills, Liston O. "Pastoral Care: History, Tradition, and Definitions." In *Dictionary of Pastoral Care and Counseling,* ed. Rodney J. Hunter, 836-844. Nashville: Abingdon Press, 1990.

Moore, Thomas. *Care of the Soul: A Guide for Cultivating Depth and Sacredness in Everyday Life.* New York: HarperPerennial, 1992.

Neuger, Christie C. "Women's Depression: Lives at Risk." In *Women in Travail and Transition: A New Pastoral Care,* eds. Maxine Glaz and Jeanne Stevenson Moessner, 146-161. Minneapolis: Fortress Press, 1991.

Nishitani, Keiji. *Religion and Nothingness.* Trans. Jan Van Bragt. Berkeley: University of California Press, 1982.

Nolen-Hoeksema, Susan. *Sex Differences in Depression.* Stanford: Stanford University Press, 1990.

Noll, Katherine M., John M. Davis, and Frank DeLeon-Jones. "Medication and Somatic Therapies in the Treatment of Depression." In *Handbook of Depression: Treatment, Assessment, and Research,* eds. Ernest E. Beckham and William R. Leber, 220-315. Homewood, IL: Dorsey Press, 1985.

O'Hearne, John J., and Richard Dayringer. "Transactional Analysis Dealing with Depression." In *Dealing with Depression: Five Pastoral Interventions,* ed. Richard Dayringer, 13-26. Binghamton, NY: The Haworth Pastoral Press, 1995.

Panikkar, Raimundo. *Myth, Faith and Hermeneutics: Cross-Cultural Studies.* New York: Paulist Press, 1979.

Peterson, Christopher, Steven F. Maier, Martin E. P. Seligman. *Learned Helplessness: A Theory for the Age of Personal Control.* New York: Oxford University Press, 1993.

Propst, Rebecca L. *Psychotherapy in a Religious Framework: Spirituality in the Emotional Healing Process.* New York: Human Sciences Press, 1988.

Pyszczynski, Tom, and Jeff Greenberg. *Hanging On and Letting Go: Understanding the Onset, Progression, and Remission of Depression.* New York: Springer-Verlag, 1992.

Rehm, Lynn P., and Mary J. Naus, "A Memory Model of Emotion." In *Contemporary Psychological Approaches to Depression: Theory, Research, and Treatment,* ed. Rick E. Ingram, 23-35. New York: Plenum Press, 1988.

Rohr, Richard. *Simplicity: The Art of Living.* Trans. Peter Heinegg. New York: Crossroad Publishing, 1991.

Rosen, David. *Transforming Depression: Healing the Soul Through Creativity.* New York: Penguin Books, 1993.

Rubin, Jeffery. *Psychotherapy and Buddhism: Toward an Integration.* New York: Plenum Press, 1996.

Rush, A. John. "Diagnosis of Affective Disorder." In *Depression: Basic Mechanisms, Diagnosis, and Treatment,* eds. A. John Rush and Kenneth Z. Altshuler, 1-31. New York: Guilford Press, 1986.

Sartre, Jean Paul. *Being and Nothingness: A Phenomenological Essay on Ontology.* Trans. Hazel E. Barnes. New York: Washington Square Press, 1956.

Scheier, Michael F., and Charles S. Carver. "Individual Differences in Self-Concept and Self-Process." In *The Self in Social Psychology,* eds. Daniel M. Wegner and Robin R. Vallacher, 229-251. New York: Oxford University Press, 1980.

Schlesser, Michael A. "Neuroendocrine Abnormalities in Affective Disorders." In *Depression: Basic Mechanisms, Diagnosis, and Treatment,* eds. A. John Rush and Kenneth Z. Altshuler, 45-71. New York: Guilford Press, 1986.

Scully, James H. *Psychiatry.* Media, PA: Harwal Publishing, 1985.

Seligman, Martin E. P. "Why Is There So Much Depression Today? The Waxing of the Individual and the Waning of the Commons." In *Contemporary Psychological Approaches to Depression: Theory, Research, and Treatment,* ed. Rick E. Ingram, 1-9. New York: Plenum Press, 1990.

Song, Choan Seng. *Theology from the Womb of Asia.* Maryknoll, NY: Orbis Books, 1986.

Stambaugh, Joan. "Heidegger, Taoism, and the Question of Metaphysics." In *Heidegger and Asian Thought,* ed. Graham Parkes, 79-91. Honolulu: University of Hawaii Press, 1987.

Stcherbatsky, Fedor Ippolitovich. *The Central Conception of Buddhism.* New Delhi: Motilal Banarsidass, 1922.

Stone, Howard. Depression and Hope: New Insights for Pastoral Counseling. Minneapolis: Fortress Press, 1998.

_____. "Depression." In *Handbook for Basic Types of Pastoral Care and Counseling,* eds. Howard Stone and William M. Clements, 179-208. Nashville: Abingdon Press, 1991.

Styron, William. *Darkness Visible: A Memoir of Madness.* New York: Vintage Books, 1990.

Suzuki, Daisetz Teitaro. Introduction to *The Text of Taoism.* Trans. James Legge. New York: Julian Press, 1959.

Tillich, Paul. *Courage to Be*. Glasgov: Collins, 1957.

_____. *Systematic Theology*, Vol. 1. London: SCM, 1951-1957.

_____. *Systematic Theology*, Vol. 2. London: SCM, 1951-1957.

Tortora, Gerald J. *Principles of Human Anatomy*. New York: HarperCollins Publishers, 1992.

Watson, Burton, Trans. Introduction to *Chuang Tzu: Basic Writings*, by Burton Watson. New York: Columbia University Press, 1996.

Watts, Alan. *Tao: The Watercourse Way*. New York: Pantheon Books, 1963.

Wicklund, Robert, and Dieter Frey. "Self-awareness Theory: When the Self Makes a Difference." In *The Self in Social Psychology*, eds. Daniel M. Wegner and Robin R. Vallacher, 31-54. New York: Oxford University Press, 1980.

Williams, J. Mark G. *The Psychological Treatment of Depression: A Guide to the Theory and Practice of Cognitive-Behavior Therapy*. New York: Free Press, 1984.

Wing, John, and Paul Bebbington. "Epidemiology of Depression." In *Handbook of Depression: Treatment, Assessment and Research*, eds. Ernest Edward Beckham and William Leber, 765-794. Homewood, IL: Dorsey Press, 1985.

Wu, Kuang-ming. *Chuang Tzu: World Philosopher at Play*. New York: Crossroad Publishing, 1982.

Journals

Abramson, Lyn Y., Martin E. Seligman, and John D. Teasdale. "Learned Helplessness in Humans: Critique and Reformation." *Journal of Abnormal Psychology* 87 (1978): 65-66.

Alloy, Lauren B., and Anthony H. Ahrens. "Depression and Pessimism for the Future: Biased Use of Statistically Relevant Information in Predictions for Self Versus Others." *Journal of Personality and Social Psychology* 41 (1987): 366-378.

Beaman, Arthur L., Bonnel Klentz, Edward Diener, and Soren Svanum. "Objective Self-Awareness and Transgression in Children: A Field Study." *Journal of Personality and Social Psychology* 37 (1979): 1835-1846.

Beck, Aaron T., Gary Brown, Robert Steer, Judy I. Eidelson, and John H. Riskind. "Differentiating Anxiety and Depression: A Test of the Cognitive Content Specificity Hypotheses." *Journal of Abnormal Psychology* 96 (1987): 179-183.

Belsher, Gayle, and Charles G. Costello. "Relapse After Recovery from Unipolar Depression: A Critical Review." *Psychological Bulletin* 104, no. 1 (1988): 84-96.

Billings, Andrew G., and Rudolf H. Moos. "Coping, Stress, and Social Resources Among Adults with Unipolar Depression." *Journal of Personality and Social Psychology* 46 (1984): 877-891.

Blaney, Paul H. "Affect and Memory: A Review." *Psychological Bulletin* 99 (1986): 229-246.

Boyd, Jeffrey, and Myrna Weissman. "Epidemiology of Affective Disorders." *Archives of General Psychiatry* 38 (1981): 1039-1046.

Bringle, Mary Louise. " 'I Just Can't Stop Thinking about It': Depression, Rumination, and Forgiveness." *Word and World* 16, no. 3 (1996): 340-346.

_____. "Soul-Dye and Salt: Integrating Spiritual and Medical Understandings of Depression." *Journal of Pastoral Care* 50, no. 4 (1996), 329-339.

Buchwald, Alexander M. "Depressive Mood and Estimates of Reinforcement Frequency." *Journal of Abnormal Psychology* 86 (1977): 443-446.

Clark, David M., and John D. Teasdale. "Diurnal Variation in Clinical Depression and Accessibility of memories of Positive and Negative Experiences." *Journal of Abnormal Psychology* 91 (1982): 87-95.

Coyne, James C. "Depression and the Response of Others." *Journal of Abnormal Psychology* 85 (1976): 186-193.

Crook, Thomas, Allen Raskin, and John Eliot. "Parent-Child Relationships and Adult Depression." *Child Development* 52 (1981): 950-957.

Diener, Edward, and Thomas K. Srull. "Self-Awareness, Psychological Perspective, and the Self-Reinforcement in Relation to Personal and Social Standards." *Journal of Personality and Social Psychology* 37 (1979): 413-423.

Diener, Edward, and Mark C. Wallbom. "Effects of Self-Awareness on Anti-Normative Behavior." *Journal of Research in Personality* 10 (1976): 107-111.

Dobson, Keith S., and Brian F. Shaw. "Specificity and Stability of Self-Referent Encoding in Clinical Depression." *Journal of Abnormal Psychology* 96 (1987): 34-40.

Friedman, Alfred S. "Minimal Effects of Severe Depression on Cognitive Functioning." *Journal of Abnormal and Social Psychology* 69 (1964): 237-243.

Gibbons, Frederick X. "Sexual Standards and Reactions to Pornography: Enhancing Behavioral Consistency Through Self-Focused Attention." *Journal of Personality and Social Psychology* 36 (1978): 976-987.

Gotlib, Ian H. "Perception and Recall of Interpersonal Feedback: Negative Bias in Depression." *Cognitive Therapy and Research* 7 (1983): 399-412.

_____. "Self-Reinforcement and Recall: Differential Deficits in Depressed and Nondepressed Psychiatric Patients." *Journal of Abnormal Psychology* 90 (1981): 521-530.

Gotlib, Ian H., and S. J. Meltzer, "Depression and the Perception of Social Skill in Dyadic Interaction." *Cognitive Therapy and Research* 11 (1987): 41-53.

Greenberg, Jeff. "Persistent High Self-Focus After Failure and Low Self-Focus After Success: The Depressive Self-Focusing Style." *Journal of Personality and Social Psychology* 50, no. 5 (1986): 1039-1044.

Greenberg, Jeff, Sheldon Solomon, Mitchell Veeder, Deborah Lyon, Tom Pyszczynski, Abram Rosenblatt, and Shari Kirkland. "Evidence for Terror Management Theory II: The Effects of Mortality Salience on Reactions to Those Who Threaten or Bolster the Cultural Worldview." *Journal of Personality and Social Psychology* 58, no. 2 (1990): 308-318.

Greenfield, Shelly F., Roger D. Weiss, Larry R. Muenz, Lisa M. Vagge, John F. Kelly, Lisa R. Bello, and Jacqueline Michael. "The Effect of Depression on Return to Drinking: A Prospective Study." *Archive of General Psychiatry* 55, no. 3 (1998): 259-265.

Hammen, Constance, and Susan E. Krantz, "Effect of Success and Failure on Depressive Cognition." *Journal of Abnormal Psychology* 85 (1976): 577-586.

Harmon-Jones, Eddie, Linda Simon, Jeff Greenberg, Tom Pyszczynski, Sheldon Solomon, and Holly McGregor. "Terror Management Theory and Self-Esteem: Evidence That Increased Self-Esteem Reduces Mortality Salience Effects." *Journal of Personality and Social Psychology* 72, no. 1 (1997): 24-36.

Harris, Tirril, George W. Brown, and A. Bifulco. "Loss of Parent in Childhood and Adult Psychiatric Disorder: The Role of Lack of Adequate Parental Care." *Psychological Medicine* 16 (1986): 641-659.

Holahan, Charles J., and Rudolph H. Moos. "Life Stressors, Personal and Social Resources, and Depression: A 4-Year Structural Model." *Journal of Abnormal Psychology* 100 (1991): 31-38

Ilfeld, Frederic W. "Current Social Stressors and Symptoms of Depression." *American Journal of Psychiatry* 134 (1977): 161-166.

Ingram, Rick E., and T. W. Smith. "Depression and Internal versus External Focus of Attention." *Cognitive Therapy and Research* 8 (1984): 139-152.

Keller, Martin B., Philip W. Lavori, Jean Endicott, William Coryell, and Gerald L. Klerman. "Double Depression: Two-Year Follow-Up." *American Journal of Psychiatry* 44 (1983): 689-694.

Keller, Martin B., Robert W. Shapiro, Philip W. Lavori, and Nicola Wolfe. "Relapse in Major Depressive Disorder." *Archives of General Psychiatry* 39 (1982): 911-915.

Klerman, Gerald L., Philip W. Lavori, John Rice, Theodore Reich, Jean Endicott, Nancy C. Andreasen, Martin B. Keller, and Robert M. A. Hirschfield. "Birth Cohort Trends in Rates of Major Depressive Disorder Among Relatives of Patients with Affective Disorder." *Archieves of General Psychiatry* 42 (1985): 689-693.

Klerman, Gerald L., and Myrna M. Weissman. "Course, Morbidity, and Costs of Depression." *Archives of General Psychiatry* 49 (1992): 831-834.

Kuiper, Nicholas A. "Depression and Causal Attributions for Success and Failure." *Journal of Personality and Social Psychology* 36 (1978): 236-246.

Lewinsohn, Peter M., Edward M. Duncan, Alyn K. Stanton, and Martin Hautzinger. "Age at First Onset for Nonbipolar Depression." *Journal of Abnormal Psychology* 95 (1986): 378-383.

Lewinhson, Peter M., H. M. Hoberman, and M. Rosenbaum. "A Prospective Study of Risk Factors for Unipolar Depression." *Journal of Abnormal Psychology* 97 (1988): 251-264.

Li, Chenyang. "What-Being: Chuang Tzu versus Aristotle." *International Philosophical Quarterly* 33, no. 3 (1993): 341-353.

Linville, Patricia W. "Self-Complexity As a Cognitive Buffer Against Stress-Related Illness and Depression." *Journal of Personality and Social Psychology* 52 (1987): 663-676.

National Institute of Mental Health/National Institute of Health (IMH/NIH) Consensus Development Conference Statement. "Mood Disorders: Pharmacologic Prevention of Recurrences." *American Journal of Psychiatry* 142 (1985): 469-476.

Neylan, T. C. "Treatment of Sleep Disturbances in Depressed Patients." *Journal of Clinical Psychiatry* 56, no. 2 (1995): 56-61.

Nolen-Hoeksema, Susan. "Sex Differences in Unipolar Depression: Evidence and Theory." *Psychological Bulletin* 101 (1987): 259-282.

Nolen-Hoeksema, Susan, Joan S. Girgus, and Martin E. P. Seligman. "Sex Differences in Depression and Explanatory Style in Children." *Journal of Youth and Adolescence* 20, no. 2 (1991), 233-245.

Odens, M. L. and C. H. Fox. "Adult Sleep Apnea Syndromes." *American Family Physician* 52, no. 3 (1995): 856-866.

Pyszczynski, Tom. Letter to author, August 27, 1998.

Pyszczynski, Tom, and Jeff Greenberg. "Depression and Preference for Self-Focusing Stimuli After Success and Failure." *Journal of Personality and Social Psychology* 49, no. 4 (1985): 1066-1075.

Pyszczynski, Tom, and Jeff Greenberg. "Depressive Self-Focusing Style." *Journal of Research in Personality* 20 (1986): 96.

Pyszczynski, Tom, and Jeff Greenberg. "Evidence for a Depressive Self-Focusing Style." *Journal of Research in Personality* 20 (1986): 95-106.

Pyszczynski, Tom, James C. Hamilton, Fred H. Herring, and Jeff Greenberg. "Depression, Self-Focused Attention, and the Negative Memory Bias." *Journal of Personality and Social Psychology* 56, no. 2 (1989): 351-357.

Robins, Lee N., John E. Helzer, Myrna Weissman, Helen Orvaschel, Ernest Greenberg, Jack D. Burke, Jr., and Darrel A. Regier. "Lifetime Prevalence of Specific Psychiatric Disorders in Three Sites." *Archives of General Psychiatry* 41, no. 10 (1984): 949-958.

Robinson, Leslie A., Jeffrey S. Berman, and Robert A. Neimeyer. "Psychotherapy for the Treatment of Depression: A Comprehensive Review of Controlled Outcome Research." *Psychological Bulletin* 108, no. 1 (1990): 30-49.

Sweeney, Paul D., Karen Anderson, and Scott Bailey. "Attributional Style in Depression: A Meta-Analytic Review." *Journal of Personality and Social Psychology* 50 (1986): 974-991.

Weissman, Myrna M. "Advances in Psychiatric Epidemiology: Rates and Risks for Depression." *American Journal of Public Health* 77 (1987): 445-451.

Weissman, Myrna, and Cross-National Collaborative Group. "The Changing Rate of Major Depression." *Journal of the American Medical Association* 268, no. 21 (1992): 3098-3104.

Weissman, Myrna, and J. Myers. "Affective Disorders in a United States Urban Community: The Use of Research Diagnostic Criteria in an Epidemiological Survey." *Archives of General Psychiatry* 38 (1978): 1304-1311.

Wicklund, Robert. "Objective Self-Awareness." *Advances in Experimental Social Psychology* 8 (1975): 233-275.

Wicklund, Robert, and Shelley Duval. "Opinion Change and Performance Facilitation As a Result of Objective Self-awareness." *Journal of Experimental Social Psychology* 7 (1971): 319-342.

Wood, Joanne V., Judith A. Saltzberg, John M. Neale, Arthur A. Stone, and Tracy B. Rachmiel. "Self-Focused Attention, Coping Responses, and Distressed Mood in Everyday Life." *Journal of Personality and Social Psychology* 58, no. 6 (1990): 1027-1036.

Dissertations

Franche, Renee-Louise. "Self-Criticism and Dependency as Vulnerability Factors to Depression." PhD diss., University of British Columbia (Canada), 1991.

Giaquinto, Edward John Jr., "Depression, Self-Focused Attention and Negative Memory Bias: A Replication and Extension," PhD diss., California School of Professional Psychology (San Diego), 1995.

Pietromonaco, Paula Ray. "The Nature of the Self-Structure in Depression." PhD diss., University of Michigan, 1983. Abstract in Dissertation Abstracts International 44-10B (1983): 3243.

Sloan, Lora Lee. "Processing Strategies and Recall Performance for Narrative Passages and Word Lists of Negative and Neutral Affective Valence in Depression (Memory Deficits)." PhD diss., University of North Dakota, 1997.

Index

Order Your Own Copy of
This Important Book for Your Personal Library!

WU WEI, NEGATIVITY, AND DEPRESSION
The Principle of Non-Trying in the Practice of Pastoral Care

_____in hardbound at $49.95 (ISBN: 0-7890-1093-3)

_____in softbound at $17.95 (ISBN: 0-7890-1094-1)

COST OF BOOKS_____

OUTSIDE USA/CANADA/
MEXICO: ADD 20%_____

POSTAGE & HANDLING_____
(US: $4.00 for first book & $1.50
for each additional book)
Outside US: $5.00 for first book
& $2.00 for each additional book)

SUBTOTAL_____

in Canada: add 7% GST_____

STATE TAX_____
(NY, OH & MIN residents, please
add appropriate local sales tax)

FINAL TOTAL_____
(If paying in Canadian funds,
convert using the current
exchange rate, UNESCO
coupons welcome.)

❏ **BILL ME LATER:** ($5 service charge will be added)
(Bill-me option is good on US/Canada/Mexico orders only;
not good to jobbers, wholesalers, or subscription agencies.)

❏ Check here if billing address is different from
shipping address and attach purchase order and
billing address information.

Signature_____

❏ **PAYMENT ENCLOSED: $_____**

❏ **PLEASE CHARGE TO MY CREDIT CARD.**

❏ Visa   ❏ MasterCard   ❏ AmEx   ❏ Discover
❏ Diner's Club   ❏ Eurocard   ❏ JCB

Account # _____

Exp. Date_____

Signature_____

Prices in US dollars and subject to change without notice.

NAME_____

INSTITUTION_____

ADDRESS_____

CITY_____

STATE/ZIP_____

COUNTRY_____ COUNTY (NY residents only)_____

TEL_____ FAX_____

E-MAIL_____

May we use your e-mail address for confirmations and other types of information? ❏ Yes ❏ No
We appreciate receiving your e-mail address and fax number. Haworth would like to e-mail or fax special
discount offers to you, as a preferred customer. **We will never share, rent, or exchange your e-mail address
or fax number.** We regard such actions as an invasion of your privacy.

Order From Your Local Bookstore or Directly From
The Haworth Press, Inc.
10 Alice Street, Binghamton, New York 13904-1580 • USA
TELEPHONE: 1-800-HAWORTH (1-800-429-6784) / Outside US/Canada: (607) 722-5857
FAX: 1-800-895-0582 / Outside US/Canada: (607) 722-6362
E-mail: getinfo@haworthpressinc.com
PLEASE PHOTOCOPY THIS FORM FOR YOUR PERSONAL USE.
www.HaworthPress.com

BOF00

SPIRITUAL CRISIS
Surviving Trauma to the Soul
J. LeBron McBride, PhD
"Offers nondenominational Christian aid for troubled souls going through tough times of belief transition, loss of faith, and potentially damaging extremes in living and thinking."
—Bookpaper
$49.95 hard. ISBN: 0-7890-0135-7.
$19.95 soft. ISBN: 0-7890-0460-7.
1998. 207 pp. with Index.
Features case studies, tables, and figures.

WHAT THE DYING TEACH US
Lessons on Living
Reverend Samuel Lee Oliver, BCC
"Pastoral care counselor's experiences with hospice patients and their families are life-affirming lessons of benefit to those facing death, their loved ones, and caretakers in the field."
—Bookpaper
$59.95 hard. ISBN: 0-7890-0475-5.
$17.95 soft. ISBN: 0-7890-0476-3.
1998. 128 pp. with Index.
Features personal reflections on death and dying.

UNDERSTANDING CLERGY MISCONDUCT IN RELIGIOUS SYSTEMS
Scapegoating, Family Secrets, and the Abuse of Power
Candace R. Benyei, PhD
"The coping strategies and intervention techniques that are outlined provide guidance in pinpointing the sickness at its source and restoring felicity and order to religious leadership and the community."
—Adolescence
$49.95 hard. ISBN: 0-7890-0451-8.
$19.95 soft. ISBN: 0-7890-0452-6. 1998. 197 pp. with Index.
Features a glossary and appendixes.

PASTORAL CARE IN PREGNANCY LOSS
A Ministry Long Needed
Thomas Moe, DMin
$69.95 hard. ISBN: 0-7890-0124-1.
$19.95 soft. ISBN: 0-7890-0196-9. 1997. 162 pp. with Index.